Publishing and Development:
A Book of Readings

Bellagio Studies in Publishing

Philip G. Altbach, General Editor

Other titles in this series include:

1: Philip G. Altbach, editor, *Publishing in Africa and the Third World*

2: Carol Priestley, *Publishing Assistance Programs: Review and Inventory*

3: Philip G. Altbach and Hyaeweol Choi, *Bibliography on Publishing in the Third World, 1980-1993*   (Published by Ablex Publishers, 355 Chestnut St., Norwood, NJ 07648 USA)

4: Philip G. Altbach, editor, *Copyright and Development: Inequality in the Information Age*

5: Urvashi Butalia and Ritu Menon, *Making a Difference: Feminist Publishing in the South*

6: Henry Chakava, *Publishing in Africa: One Man's Perspective*

7: Philip G. Altbach, editor, *The Challenge of the Market: Privatization and Publishing in Africa*

8: Philip G. Altbach and Damtew Teferra, editors, *Knowledge Dissemination in Africa: The Role of Scholarly Journals*

9: Philip G. Altbach and Damtew Teferra, editors, *Publishing and Development: A Book of Readings*

Publishing and Development: *A Book of Readings*

Edited by
Philip G. Altbach and Damtew Teferra

Bellagio Studies in Publishing, 9

Bellagio Publishing Network
Research and Information Center
in association with the Boston College
Center for International Higher Education
Chestnut Hill, Massachusetts USA

Published in cooperation with
Obor, The International Book Institute, Inc.

February, 1998

© 1998 Bellagio Publishing Network

For further information about this publication, please contact:

Bellagio Publishing Network
Research and Information Center
207 Campion Hall
Boston College
Chestnut Hill MA 02167, USA

Fax: (617) 552-8422

For information about the Bellagio Publishing Network, please contact:

Bellagio Publishing Network Secretariat
The Jam Factory
27 Park End St.,
Oxford OX1 1HU, UK

Fax: 44-1865-244-584

ISBN number: 0-9646078-4-0

Bellagio Studies in Publishing, 9

Copies of this book may be ordered from
African Books Collective, Ltd.
The Jam Factory
27 Park End St.
Oxford OX1 1HU, UK

Fax: 44-1865-793-298

Table of Contents

Foreword	vii
Acknowledgments	xi
Introduction: Publishing, Independence, and Development Philip G. Altbach and Damtew Teferra	xiii

1. Current Trends in Book Publishing   1
    Philip G. Altbach

2. Multinationals and Third World Publishing   17
    Gordon Graham

3. The Economics of Book Publishing   31
    Datus C. Smith, Jr.

4. International Copyright   47
    Paul Gleason

5. Distribution: The Neglected Link in the Publishing Chain   75
    Amadio A. Arboleda

6. Educational Publishing and Book Provision   91
    Pernille Askerud

7. The Transition from State to Commercial Publishing
    Systems in African Countries   111
    Paul Brickhill

8. Electronic Publishing: New Technologies and Publishing   131
    Czeslaw Jan Grycz

9. Publishing in the Third World: Issues and Trends for the
    Twenty-First Century   159
    Philip G. Altbach

Contributors   191

Foreword

Publishing for Social Change

> Development is like a tree: it can be nurtured in its growth only by feeding its roots, not by pulling on its branches.
> —Ismail Serageldin, *Nurturing Development: Aid and Cooperation in Today's Changing World*

(Editors' note: We acknowledge the assistance of Obor, The International Book Institute, Inc., in the publication of this book.)

As Philip Altbach and Damtew Teferra have noted, publishing—the spreading of ideas in accessible written form—can be a key contributor to independence and development. Indeed, it would be hard to overstate the role that books—in the language of their intended audience and widely distributed in inexpensive formats—can play in promoting ideas that may effect or impact social change. However, publishing for such goals is difficult and calls for careful support from international partners.

Obor ("torch" in Indonesian) is one of the oldest organizations in the United States supporting specialized international publishing. It was established in 1970 to help the people of Indonesia form a nongovernmental organization (NGO) to select important books to be published in Jakarta in the national language, Bahasa Indonesia. From this simple beginning, Obor has become a small but serious force internationally for intellectual freedom and a chapter in the history of ideas.

Conceived, established, nurtured, and managed for more than a quarter century by Ivan Kats, Obor has retained its original mission to stimulate the international flow of important ideas by encouraging the translation, publication, and distribution of books in languages in which they might otherwise not appear. Today, as in 1970, Obor continues to support the establishment and growth of small, independent book publishing organizations in developing countries—organizations that would be unable, initially, to succeed commercially without outside assistance.

The way Obor functions, though closely related to other such organizations, is unique as far as we know. While many other organizations work to support the development and flourishing of publishers around the world, Obor helps interested individuals in a given country to work directly with established publishers by establishing a NGO to produce important new works. As an experienced international partner, Obor is supporting the emergence of a new entity in civic society. Obor serves as bibliographic consultant, publishing adviser, fundraiser, and management consultant. Its constant goal is the development of a suitable new organ in society that can function independently of Obor.

Obor's raison d'être remains serving the affiliate organizations' two dimensions of work. First, their efforts in selecting and publishing quality books around the world helps those societies modernize and humanize their ideas and outlooks. To date, Obor has affiliates in five countries of operation (Indonesia, Pakistan, Thailand, Vietnam, and Morocco) and collaborating partners in five other countries (Kenya, Bangladesh, the Philippines, Sri Lanka, and Malaysia) have published 600 works, nearly 25 percent of them in the last two years. Second, and equally important, is that the affiliates' work—as NGOs where laws permit, as individuals or informal associations elsewhere—makes them instruments in and of emerging civic societies.

In the last two years, Obor has undertaken changes that will further institutionalize its work and prepare the organization for the future. Now based in Philadelphia, with an expanded board, new management, and new name—Obor, The International Book Institute—the organization is working to deepen and, perhaps, broaden its activities. Obor has worked with its original and largest affiliate, Yayasan Obor Indonesia (YOI), to support the affiliate's full independence from its founder, Obor. YOI has now received a final two-year grant from USAID, which for a number of years has funded Obor's assistance to its partner in Indonesia. Obor serves as a subcontractor to its Indonesian partner, which is now almost fully self-sustaining. This signal accomplishment by Obor's Indonesian partner is most exciting. "We are breaking through to independence," says Mochtar Lubis, "and we now believe we can be truly self-sustaining through our own sales and fundraising efforts." Obor has been developing and implementing a publishing training program, at YOI's request, in cooperation with the Canadian Centre for Publishing Studies, at Simon Fraser University, in Vancouver, British Columbia. This may serve as a model for other Obor affiliates and supporters of independent publishing, who will be informed about the training program at their 1998 international gathering in Jakarta.

Responding to Obor's request for a volume of readings to assist in worldwide efforts to support publishing in developing countries, the editors have addressed and illuminated many of the issues affecting books and publishing. Whether from the current Obor network, the Bellagio Network to which Obor belongs, the Central European University in Budapest, or other agencies, those who work to advance autonomous publishing will find much in this volume to support, challenge, and deepen their thinking.

Obor would like to express its appreciation to editors Philip G. Altbach and Damtew Teferra for their work on this volume. Finally, Obor would like to thank La Fondation Charles Léopold Mayer pour le Progrès de l'Homme (fph) for its assistance. Michel Sauquet of this action-oriented foundation, based in Paris, has been active in his leadership and support for this project, far beyond the estimable financial support he and the foundation have made possible.

For further information, please contact:

Obor, The International Book Institute, Inc.
1501 Cherry Street
Philadelphia, PA 19144, USA
Telephone: (1) 215-636-0505
Fax: (1) 215-636-0705
e-mail: info@obor.org (office)
dkanderton@obor.org (director)
Website: http://www.obor.org

Donna K. Anderton
Executive Director, Obor
The International Book Institute, Inc.

Acknowledgments

The idea for this volume stems from a conversation with Ivan Kats, founding director of the Obor Foundation. The project was supported by his successor, Donna Anderton, who was enthusiastic about a book of key readings on publishing and development taken from the existing literature. She obtained some assistance from La Fondation Charles Léopold Mayer pour le Progrès de l'Homme. This book is cosponsored by Obor—The International Book Institute and the Bellagio Publishing Network.

This volume provides a selection of readings on the broad topic of publishing and development. Our concept is that this book will form the core of additional volumes in some of the languages of developing countries that will focus on publishing issues. The subsequent volumes will include specially prepared essays dealing with specific countries and regions.

We are indebted to the publishers who have permitted us to reprint the chapters in this book. We especially appreciate the assistance of Marie Ellen Larcada of Garland Publishing, Inc., New York, who worked with us on *International Book Publishing: An Encyclopedia*. We dedicate this volume to two of our friends who have helped to pioneer the study of the role of books in developing countries, and especially in Africa: Henry Chakava and Hans M. Zell. These visionary colleagues have contributed greatly to the development of indigenous publishing as well.

The chapters in this volume are reprinted, with permission, from the following sources:

Chapter 1. "Current Trends in Book Publishing," from Yves Courrier, ed., *World Information Yearbook, 1997–1998* (Paris: UNESCO Publishing, 1997) © UNESCO Publishing.

Chapter 2. "Multinationals and Third World Publishing," from Philip G. Altbach, ed., *Publishing and Development in the Third World* (Oxford: Hans Zell Publishers, 1992) © Hans Zell Publishers, an inprint of Bowker-Saur, a Reed-Elsevier Company.

Chapter 3. "The Economics of Book Publishing," from Datus C. Smith, Jr., *A Guide to Book Publishing* (revised ed.) (Seattle: University of Washington Press, 1989) © University of Washington Press.

Chapter 4. "International Copyright," from P. G. Altbach and E. S. Hoshino, eds. *International Book Publishing: An Encyclopedia* (New York: Garland, 1995), revised for this book. © Garland Publishing, Inc., a member of the Taylor & Francis Group.

Chapter 5. "Distribution: The Neglected Link in the Publishing Chain," from P. G. Altbach, A. A. Arboleda, and S. Gopinathan, eds., *Publishing in the Third World: Knowledge and Development* (Portsmouth, N.H.: Heinemann, 1985) © Heinemann Publishers.

Chapter 6. "Educational Publishing and Book Provision," from Pernille Askerud, *A Guide to Sustainable Book Provision* (Paris: UNESCO, 1997) © UNESCO and DANIDA.

Chapter 7. "The Transition from State to Commercial Publishing Systems in African Countries," from Philip G. Altbach, ed., *The Challenge of the Market: Privatization and Publishing in Africa* (Chestnut Hill, Mass.: Bellagio Publishing Network, 1996) © Bellagio Publishing Network.

Chapter 8. "New Technologies and Publishing," from P. G. Altbach and E. S. Hoshino, eds. *International Book Publishing: An Encyclopedia* (New York: Garland, 1995), revised for this book. © Garland Publishing, Inc., a member of the Taylor & Francis Group.

Chapter 9. "Publishing in the Third World: Issues and Trends for the Twenty-First Century," from P. G. Altbach and E. S. Hoshino, eds. *International Book Publishing: An Encyclopedia* (New York: Garland, 1995) © Garland Publishing, Inc., a member of the Taylor & Francis Group.

Introduction

Publishing, Independence, and Development

Philip G. Altbach and Damtew Teferra

This book provides a selection of key readings concerning book publishing in the developing world. Too often, in this age of multinational corporations and high technology, the needs of a small industry like publishing in low per capita income countries are forgotten. This is unfortunate as publishing remains central to these countries' educational systems, to the creation and distribution of knowledge, and to the nurturing of an independent intellectual culture. Without books and other published material, a civil society cannot exist, educational systems suffer, and knowledge cannot be communicated. Publishing is situated at the center of a complex web of communication, and is necessarily related to the whole world of ideas and knowledge.

An indigenous publishing industry remains as crucial as ever. While truly independent publishing is impossible in this interdependent world, autonomy in publishing is important if a nation, especially a developing one, is to achieve some control over the communication of relevant ideas and knowledge. The struggle between independence and dependence is necessarily part of the reality of publishing in developing nations. In the world of the twenty-first century, independence is increasingly difficult to maintain. Even in the United States, the largest publishing conglomerate is today owned by a German company. Constant awareness of the challenges to indigenous publishing is the price of maintaining a publishing industry with a degree of local control in the contemporary world.

This volume shows the great variation in the development of publishing across what we generally call the developing world. India, which is considered to be a developing country, is a major supplier of books to many African countries and also exports books to the West. Egypt is the major source of published materials in the Arab world. Zimbabwe now holds the fastest world record for producing a book.

Its bookfair has also attracted numerous publishers from around the world. On the other hand, many developing countries do not even have a national book policy. We therefore use the term "developing countries" as referring to nations with low per capita income levels. In many developing countries, publishing has certain common elements, which will be discussed in this book.

Publishing has been undergoing a technological revolution perhaps unprecedented since the invention of movable type, first in China and then, 500 years ago, in Germany. The advent of reprography, computer-assisted book production, and most recently of the Internet, have all had profound effects on publishing. In the West, some predict the demise of the traditional book as communication increasingly shifts to the Internet. Even if these dire predictions are not justified, there is no question but that the new technologies are profoundly affecting publishing. The impact has been less dramatic in the developing nations, but there too these changes are inevitable. In many ways, developing nations are at a considerable disadvantage: they have inferior technological infrastructures, they do not own the companies that control technological innovations, and their home markets for books and other knowledge products tend to be relatively small—thus eliminating the possibility of economies of scale. Even more than with traditional publishing, it is likely that ownership and control of the new technologies will be in the hands of large corporations in the industrialized nations.

The most lucrative market in Third World publishing is textbook production. For many historical, political, cultural, and economic reasons, this sector has been dominated by governments in many developing countries, especially in Africa. Due to a lack of awareness of the role of publishing, inadequate technical and managerial expertise, and the daunting bureaucracy afflicting the government offices that regulate infrastructure, the potential of publishing in the task of nation building has not been properly exploited. In addition, current developments in world trade and economic integration are incompatible with government control over publishing. One thing is certain, the era of state-dominated publishing is over. The influence of multinational publishers and the growth of indigenous publishers will probably be the main forces shaping publishing in the immediate future.

Governments will continue to play a role in publishing. Education, which includes the supply of books and reading materials to students, is the responsibility of government in most developing countries. Owing to their purchasing power as well as their control over educational policy, governments generally decide in which language, in what form, and in what volume educational materials are published. By withdrawing from their dominating position in the market, governments could play a positive role in fostering the development of indigenous publishing based on competition.

Developing countries like India, Indonesia, and Nigeria have 110, 300, and 350 languages, respectively. The vast number of languages in these countries complicates the problem of publishing. It is extremely difficult to cater to every language in these countries given their poor publishing infrastructure. As a result, language has become a politically sensitive topic in many developing countries as leaders have resorted to using languages imparted to them by their former colonizers. Governments then have a very important and decisive role to play in supporting publishing, especially for minority groups, as part of promoting the cultural heritage of the nation.

Publishing is both an art and a business. Publishing must be run on business principles if it is to survive. This basic financial principle, we hope, will permeate the publishing institutions in developing countries. At the same time, publishing has to do with ideas, and is at its core an exercise in communication. Publishers deal with authors— among the most creative people in any society. One of the problems of modern publishing is that it is increasingly forced to think only of the "bottom line," sometimes at the expense of the less commercial elements of the book business. Although it is true that publishing cannot return to an earlier, more relaxed period, the notion that publishing is about ideas and communication, as well as about profits, must be kept in mind, especially in the context of developing nations.

Maintaining autonomy in an increasingly interdependent world is a special problem for developing countries. Control over technology, the copyright system, international distribution of books and knowledge products, and capital remains rooted in the West. Because developing countries constitute a small market, those who control the knowledge industries have little interest in them. In this context, developing countries might benefit from current world trade practices by assuming an "if you can't beat them, join them" attitude. India, China and many other developing countries in Asia have done this very effectively. These countries are not major centers of knowledge production, but are growing as major stakeholders in the equation of book manufacture and distribution.

Publishing in many developing countries has been supported by numerous non-governmental organizations, among which the World Bank is the most prominent. The support extended by these organizations has had a mixed effect. Many contend, for example, that the present arrangement of World Bank support schemes should be revisited to bring them into line with the current movement toward privatization and commercialization taking place in most of the developing world.

We have chosen to highlight what we consider key and critical topics relating to publishing in the developing world. The issues discussed here are all relevant to the development and sustenance of publishing industries in developing countries. We have featured material of general interest. This book purposely focuses on broader issues and trends of publishing in developing countries. It is not a "how-to" guide to publishing, but is rather a collection of readings that examine publishing in relation to social, political, economic, and cultural factors within a society, as well as internationally. We hope the reader will benefit from a broader perspective and that, on the basis of these ideas, it will be possible to consider practical solutions to the problems highlighted here.

The challenges facing book publishing in developing nations are numerous, complex, and daunting. We hope that this book will provide thoughtful discussion of central issues of publishing in the developing world.

1
Current Trends in Book Publishing
Philip G. Altbach

Books remain a primary means of communicating knowledge. They are central to providing information, entertainment, analysis, and education to millions worldwide. In 1991, UNESCO statistics indicate that 863,000 separate titles were published worldwide. There are, in addition, more than 9,000 daily newspapers, and at least 20,000 periodicals that focus on science and scholarship. Despite the advent of new technologies for knowledge distribution, such as the Internet and other computer-based innovations, traditional books and newspapers are the primary source of information. And while the new technologies will become more important in an increasingly complex mix of knowledge distribution arrangements, the traditional book is in no danger of disappearing. Indeed, the number of titles published continues to increase steadily. For most of the world, the new technologies will not be widespread for decades if not longer, and books are and will remain the sole means of access to information. This essay focuses primarily on book publishing and will discuss the nature of the publishing enterprise as well as current challenges facing publishing worldwide. Although fairly insignificant in terms of economic impact, publishing is of central importance to the cultural, intellectual, and educational life of a nation. The development and dissemination of knowledge products is a matter of the utmost importance for any civilization.

Technological change is having an impact on publishing that is unrivaled since the industrial revolution affected the composition and printing of books—and permitted a mass market for books to emerge. At that time, in the nineteenth century in Europe and North America, rates of literacy also rose and incomes increased to create an unprecedented market for books. The strengthening of copyright, and the expansion of bookstores and public libraries resulted from an important combination of factors.

It can be argued that the end of the twentieth century is seeing a similarly profound transformation of publishing. A combination of technological factors, linked in different ways to the computer as well as to new developments in reprography, is changing the industry. Economic changes, including the multinationalization of major publishing firms, and the linking of publishing to other knowledge and entertainment industries, are also altering the landscape of books and publishing.

Books are the oldest communications technology, dating back to Johannes Gutenberg's invention of movable type in 1455.[1] Books have many advantages: they are portable, and do not require any sophisticated technology to access. The technologies needed to produce books, such as printing presses and composing equipment, are widely available, not very expensive, and are within the reach of most countries. Similarly, paper and other raw materials needed for book production are in general readily available, although the price for the quality of paper needed for printing books tends to fluctuate greatly. New technological innovations, such as computer-assisted desktop publishing, reprography, and others have reduced the cost of producing books in areas where these technologies are available. Books are also distributed fairly easily, and infrastructures for book distribution—through bookstores, direct mail, educational institutions, and the like—exist in the industrialized world. Distribution problems remain in the developing nations. While book production requires some capital, the investment needed is relatively modest, and it is possible for small publishers to get established and survive. Because of the relatively modest investment needed for book production, it is possible for limited editions to be published and small audiences to be served, although publishing for limited markets is inherently not very profitable. Book publishing is possible, although not usually very profitable, in languages used by small populations, and in unusual scripts. The traditional book is a unique product that has withstood the test of time, and will remain a primary means of communication into the future.

Our concern here is with publishing—the process of coordinating the various processes needed to bring a book from the idea in the mind of the author to a printed product available for distribution to the relevant audience. We do not deal in detail with printing, the paper industry, the legal aspects of copyright, or the technical aspects of the new computer-based innovations in composing books. Publishing, at its heart, is the coordination of the multitude of activities needed to produce books. Publishers seldom own printing presses, bookshops, or distribution agencies. Their expertise is in the selection and editing of manuscripts, and planning and supervising the process of transforming the manuscript into a book, and then ensuring that this product reaches its intended market. Marketing and sales are an essential part of the "publishing chain."

Publishing faces significant challenges at the end of the twentieth century. New technologies have transformed many of the processes of book publishing and distribution. This is true not only for composition and printing, but also for knowledge transmission itself. The Internet, for example, is becoming more central to publishing. Changes in the commercial underpinnings of publishing have significantly altered the traditional economics of the industry, especially through the consolidation of firms and the entry into publishing of multimedia corporations. Publishing has also become more international, not only through the export of knowledge products, but also in terms of multinational ownership of firms. We will focus on some of the dramatic changes in publishing that are transforming the structure of what was a traditional industry—a "profession of gentlemen." It has moved into the highly competitive commercial and technological environment of the twenty-first century.

In economic terms, publishing is of limited importance. The total turnover of the publishing industries of major industrial nations ranks below many consumer-based industries, such as, for example, breakfast cereals. Yet, publishing is of immense cultural and educational importance. It is also a central element in the emerging nexus of knowledge industries that are so important to postindustrial societies. It is not surprising, therefore, that the international regulation of knowledge industries was an important and controversial part of the recently concluded negotiations that led to the formation of the World Trade Organization (WTO). Issues relating to the piracy of knowledge products, including books, were at the heart of a highly visible trade dispute between China and the United States. French concerns about cultural penetration by foreign countries contributed to special arrangements within the context of WTO regulations.

The creation and ownership of knowledge products are of increasing importance because of the centrality of information and knowledge to postindustrial economies. Copyright, for example, emerged in seventeenth-century England as a means of protecting authors and publishers of books. The concept has broadened to include other knowledge products, including computer programs, films, and others. Books remain an important element of knowledge creation and ownership.

Copyright has emerged as one of the most important means of regulating the international flow of ideas and knowledge-based products, and is a central product for the knowledge industries of the twenty-first century. Those who control copyright have a significant advantage in the emerging knowledge-based global economy. The fact is that copyright ownership is largely in the hands of the major industrialized nations and of the major multimedia corporations—placing low per capita income countries as well as smaller economies at a significant disadvantage.

Center and Peripheries in the Knowledge System

Books and publishing are not equally distributed throughout the world. A small number of countries and languages dominate world publishing, creating patterns of considerable inequality in world publishing. The United States, the United Kingdom, Japan, France, and Germany are among the top publishing countries. These nations, joined by Russia, Spain, China, India, Egypt, and several others are responsible for a significant proportion of the world's book production. A few smaller countries produce large numbers of book titles when compared to their populations. Denmark and Israel, for example, produce more titles per capita than such major publishing nations as the United States or France. The United States, United Kingdom, France, and to some extent Spain are especially important in world publishing, since they publish in languages used internationally, and the majority of the major multinational publishers are based in these countries. These countries constitute the main international centers of publishing, and have considerable influence beyond their borders.

There is a second rank of countries with active and in some cases powerful publishing industries. Germany, Italy, and Japan, for example, are major publishing nations, ranking in the top ten in terms of annual title production. All three countries have major multinational publishers that have a global reach. The largest publisher in the United States is German-owned Bertelsmann Verlag, which controls a number of major U.S. publishers. The Italian publisher Mondadori, is an important influence in Spanish and Latin American publishing, and such Japanese publishers as Kodansha have an international reach. The export potential for books in German, Italian, and Japanese is, however, limited. These three countries have fully independent and autonomous publishing industries, and while they are affected by some trends from the major world centers of publishing—for example, bestsellers from the United States often appear on the lists of these countries—rarely does this influence work in the opposite direction.

A third category of publishing nations is made up of several large, relatively low-income producers of books. These countries tend to be more dependent on the major industrialized publishing nations, and in some cases serve as regional centers with strong ties abroad. China, India, Egypt, Mexico, and Argentina fall into this category. All have strong local publishing industries with all of the infrastructures of book production—publishers, printers, paper supplies, etc. All except China have strong markets for their books beyond their borders. Egypt, Mexico and Argentina are especially important as regional centers that have strong export markets. Egypt, for example, is the dominant publisher of books in Arabic, and the rest of the Arabic-speaking world depends on Egyptian books. Similarly, Mexico and Argentina dominate Latin American publishing in Spanish. These three countries serve as links between publishing in their respective languages and the world centers. China and India provide further variations on the theme. Their huge internal markets make them major book publishing nations. Both have modest export markets as well. India, especially, exports books to other developing nations, and is a major publisher of books in English (ranking third in this category after the United States and the United Kingdom) as well as in India's fifteen indigenous languages. These countries rely to some extent on the major world centers of publishing for books to translate, and sometimes for investment capital and other resources.

Much of the rest of the world is peripheral to the major centers of publishing. Most of Africa, for example, has only limited publishing capacity. Francophone Africa, especially, depends largely on France for books of all kinds, and there are only a few local publishers. With the exception of South Africa, and to a lesser extent Nigeria and Kenya, African nations produce few books, and their publishing industries are largely limited to textbooks for schools. The situation is similar but not as desperate in smaller and quite low per capita income Asian and Latin American countries such as Laos, Bolivia, Myanmar, El Salvador, and many other nations. For a significant part of the globe, the term "book hunger," coined in the early 1970s to dramatize the situation in much of the developing world, remains valid. Low literacy rates, lack of capital for investment, and the absence of the basic infrastructures for publishing all inhibit the development of a successful book industry.

Smaller industrialized nations also find themselves dependent in terms of publishing since local markets are so small many kinds of books cannot be economically published. Wealth and high literacy rates do not guarantee a successful book industry. Even countries, such as Denmark and Sweden, that have a fairly strong local publishing industry import many books from abroad. The Netherlands, which not only has a significant domestic publishing industry, but is the headquarters for several successful multinational publishers, depends on foreign books to a significant extent.

The publishing industry must be seen in the context of a worldwide knowledge system that is characterized by considerable inequality. Population, literacy rates, the use of a "world language," income levels, the existence of publishing infrastructures, and a history of active publishing all contribute to determining the strength of a publishing industry. Patterns of worldwide ownership of publishers and other knowledge-based firms, government policy, and flows of international trade may also contribute to the success of the publishing enterprise in a country. Centers and peripheries exist in publishing, and these relationships help to determine the place of a nation in the world of knowledge creation, distribution, and use.

Current Issues

Publishing faces a range of contemporary challenges that have a profound impact on the nature of the industry, and indirectly on the ways that books are produced and distributed. This section focuses on several of the most important issues affecting publishing today.

The Impact of New Technologies

Two basic technological developments are affecting publishing. The first is the reprographic revolution initiated by photocopy technology. This technology has stimulated not only the ubiquitous photocopy machine, bringing challenges to copyright, but has introduced innovations in printing. Computers have profoundly affected publishing in book production, distribution, and, perhaps most important in the long run, by affecting the nature of storage and retrieval of knowledge.

The reprographic revolution has been evident for several decades. At first, photocopying permitted individual readers to make copies of printed materials easily. This was followed by commercial enterprises making unauthorized copies of published material. The cost of photocopying machines and of making copies declined. Reprographic technology was soon harnessed to printing. This permitted significant economies in printing costs, especially for limited press runs. Suddenly, it was economically feasible to print small numbers of books for specialized audiences. It became possible to print books in languages spoken by small populations. Recent reprographic advances, linked to computer composition, permit even greater economies in the production of printed materials. Presses based on advanced photocopy technology can economically print small numbers of books very quickly and inexpensively. It is even possible to print single copies for individual users through this technological application.

At first seen as a challenge to traditional publishing, the reprographic revolution was successfully exploited by publishers. Problems remain, but overall the publishing industry has accommodated to new developments. Reprographic technology has been linked to printing to reduce costs. The challenges to the copyright system were, and remain, considerable. Here, too, publishers have, in general, worked out ways of accommodating to the new technology. Copyright laws have been strengthened, largely through pressure by publishers, so that unauthorized photocopying has been reduced, or at least controlled, in most countries. In some countries, users of photocopies must provide payment to the copyright holder. In a few others, most notably Sweden, publishers and authors are paid a royalty based on the use of books in libraries. Using reprographical technology for printing has been a considerable advantage to publishers, and has permitted publishing to be done on a small scale. This has assisted publishers in countries and regions, and in languages, that have only small markets. Reprographic printing is relatively inexpensive. This has permitted printing machinery based on this technology to be widely dispersed.

Of greater importance than reprography to publishing is the revolution based on the computer. Traditional composition technologies have, in much of the world, been replaced entirely by computer-based composition and book design. This has revolutionized the physical design of books and led to the development of desktop publishing, a term that refers to the creation of composed text through the use of personal computers. Sophisticated software programs exist for book preparation and design. Many languages using obscure scripts have benefited from computer-based typesetting. Computerized book design and preparation have dramatically lowered the cost of composition, and have also decentralized it. Publishers now have the capacity to carry a book through from manuscript to "camera-ready copy" prepared for printing.

The computer has also changed business procedures relating to inventory control, billing, and tracing trends in the sale of specific titles. Software programs permit publishers to reduce the cost of the business processes of publishing, allowing tasks to be performed quickly and within the firm—something that in earlier periods constituted a significant expense. This application of computer technology has also enabled small publishers to operate efficiently in ways that in earlier times could only be done by large firms through economies of scale. Computer technology has also permitted the effective use of targeted mailing lists, specialized publicity campaigns, and the like.

A final and tremendously important use of computer technology is in the area of the delivery of printed material to readers. This area of the application of technology, linking computers to the Internet as well as other alternative means of document delivery, has profound implications for publishers. This aspect of computer-based technology is in a relatively early stage of use, but it will soon have widespread implications for publishers, libraries, and bookstores. It is possible to deliver documents through electronic mail, and publishers are developing the technologies to supply materials this way. Some scientific journals are already distributed exclusively on the Internet, and publishers are increasingly using the World Wide Web and other electronic means to publicize books and journals. Aside from the technological challenges involved, there are a range of problems associated with this technology. The impact for copyright of Internet transmission remains controversial—as well as unclear. The means of obtaining payment are not yet fully defined. The use of library and other networks for distributing published material is a related issue, raising copyright and economic challenges for publishers. The problems the new technologies create regarding copyright and financing are complex but the information industry is currently developing solutions that will permit new means of access to published material.

The traditional role of the publisher in this new technological universe may change as the definition of the book is altered, and the means of distributing knowledge is linked to new technologies. Without question, the technological innovations are of profound importance to publishers and to the book industry.

THE CONTROL OF PUBLISHING

Publishing is undergoing unprecedented economic change. There is a clear trend toward consolidation in the publishing industry as large publishing firms acquire smaller ones and as media corporations move into publishing. Large publishers in the major industrialized countries have in the past two decades become giant multinational firms. Bertelsmann Verlag of Germany now owns publishers in most European nations and in the United States, and is in fact the largest producer of books in the United States. Hachette in France, Mondadori in Italy, Reed in Britain, and Elsevier and Kluwer (which merged in 1997 into the world's largest publisher of scientific journals) in the Netherlands are examples of publishers that have a worldwide presence. In the United States, for example, there were 573 mergers and acquisitions in the publishing industry between 1960 and 1989. Over half of the market share of American publishing is held by the top fifteen firms. Other major industrialized nations show similar trends.

The multinational publishers have also moved into smaller book markets, purchasing firms and establishing branches. These firms, because of their economic and staff resources, and their global reach, can come to dominate publishing in many developing countries. For example, French publishers have traditionally held a powerful position in Francophone Africa, and British firms are re-entering some of the Anglophone African markets that they abandoned in the years following the end of colonialism.

At the same time, new technologies, the development of "niche markets" that had been abandoned by the large firms, and increasing specialization in the book industry have permitted small firms to survive and even prosper in a market increasingly dominated by giant multinational companies. The small publishers can make use of desktop technology, computer-based direct marketing, and new printing arrangements that permit economical, limited printing. This situation also has potential for publishers in small markets, and for publishers in developing countries, although limited access to the new technologies hinders success in developing areas.

COPYRIGHT

A detailed analysis of current copyright issues is not possible here, but it is important to note that copyright has special importance to book publishing at this time. While traditional copyright is more widely accepted than ever internationally, and the piracy of books is, comparatively speaking, at a low level, technology and the multinationalization of publishing have created significant challenges for copyright. While books continue to be pirated in a small number of developing countries without significant publishing industries, virtually all countries have joined the main international copyright agreements, and generally observe copyright. Nations, such as India, that at one time were critics of traditional copyright and engaged in some book piracy, now support copyright, in part because a local publishing industry has developed that benefits from copyright protection. Among major publishing nations, it seems that only in China is there significant book piracy, and even there compliance is increasing.

Copyright, of course, protects the owners of intellectual property and sometimes makes it difficult for people in countries that have limited purchasing power and few publishing resources to obtain access to books. Copyright, in this respect, reinforces a system of knowledge inequality and creates a kind of monopoly dominated by the owners of knowledge. The copyright system works against those who have least to spend on books and other knowledge products and those who are consumers rather than producers.

We have seen a strengthening of the copyright system. Publishers in the industrialized nations are increasingly insistent on protecting their rights, and their economic benefits. There is little willingness to permit "have not" nations special access to books. The recent negotiations that established the WTO provided special protection to knowledge products and further strengthened copyright.

The challenges to copyright relate to the difficulty of enforcing copyright through the Internet and other emerging means of communicating information. Electronic networks require new approaches to the idea of copyright and new ways of enforcing the ownership of intellectual property. Just as the photocopy machine required the development of new ideas such as "fair use" as a means of defining what is subject to copyright protection, and new enforcement mechanisms to ensure both compliance and payment for use, the Internet and other innovations necessitate similar refinements in the system of copyright.

The Varieties of Publishing

It is very difficult to generalize about book publishing. It is an industry that is characterized by major variations. Publishers differ in size, scope, focus, and orientation. It is worth briefly discussing several of the major types of publishing. In most countries, textbooks constitute the largest and in many cases the dominant segment of publishing. In developing countries, textbooks form the economic basis of the entire industry, and without the text market, publishers find it difficult to survive. Indeed, textbooks and other materials published for the schools and other educational institutions constitute the large majority of books published. Publishers in industrialized nations are less dependent on the educational market, although textbooks are important worldwide as an economic mainstay of the publishing industry.

Reference and scientific, technical and medical (STM) publishing is also a major sector of publishing. Publishing in these areas is important not only because it constitutes a major segment of the market, but because these books contribute to science, scholarship, and knowledge. Unlike textbooks, which are in general published for use within one country, reference and STM books have a wide export market. Publishing in these areas is heavily dominated by the major industrial nations, which produce most of the scientific research and which are the major markets as well. In some countries, university presses are involved in publishing in these areas while in others private specialized publishers dominate.

The publication of general books (fiction, current events, poetry, political analysis, and the like)—the kinds of books sold in most bookstores—actually constitutes a small segment of the book market in most countries. Although this segment of the industry tends to be the most prestigious and visible, it is only a minor part of the industry as a whole. These books are important because they add to the intellectual life of society. There are many other segments of the book market as well. Publishing for children, for example, has a significant market in many countries. In this area, design and artwork are important, and public libraries constitute a significant source of sales. The special characteristics of children's publishing include economic factors as well as design, distribution, and printing. Other genres, including art books, "self-help" volumes, religious books, and many others constitute "niche markets" that have unique characteristics requiring specific publishing expertise. There are many types of publishing, each facing specific conditions. All are currently experiencing significant change due to the factors that have been discussed earlier.

Patterns of ownership of publishers also vary. It has been noted that there is a trend toward consolidation in the industry, and for the emergence of large multinational firms. There is an increasing involvement of multimedia conglomerate corporations in publishing. Critics of this trend have pointed out that the personal element in publishing is being lost. There are also many small and specialized publishers in the industrialized countries—some of which are very successful due to their serving "niche" markets. In developing countries, publishers tend to be small, undercapitalized, and less specialized since the book market is small and fewer niches are available. Many publishers were established as family firms, and in developing countries remain family owned. The financial control of publishing firms determines their nature, direction, and ethos. These patterns are in the process of significant change.

The Future of the Book

Publishers face a future in which the traditional definition of the book is changing. Publishers will have to adapt to the new realities if they are to survive. Books will remain as an important product, and as a central means of imparting knowledge and entertainment. At the same time, the means of producing, distributing, and even editing books are changing. Economics, technology, and the increasing interweaving of the world economy are all affecting books and publishing.

Publishers must inevitably be more international in their outlook—we are already seeing the expansion of multinational publishing. More books are being translated, although by and large books are being translated from the major metropolitan languages to languages spoken by smaller populations, and there is relatively little translation in the other direction. The ownership of publishing firms shows similar characteristics. Major firms in the large industrialized nations expand into other parts of the world. In Africa, for example, not only are major European publishers entering the market, but better established firms with more capital from South Africa are expanding into other sub-Saharan African nations. At the same time, there is considerable scope for indigenous publishing because local publishers and entrepreneurs have the advantage of knowing national realities and are able to quickly adapt to changing circumstances. There is, without question, a rapidly changing pattern of ownership and entrepreneurship in publishing worldwide.

The book is often linked to other media products, and this will have an impact on what is published and the nature of books, perhaps even changing the definition of the books in the long run. Links between books and films, for example, are common, and books are often related to computer applications or CD ROM products. Books are increasingly issued in other forms, especially on CD ROM, adding an entirely new dimension to publishing. Publishers in the United States, Europe, and Japan are occasionally bypassing the traditional book in favor of alternative high-tech formats, a trend that is likely to grow.

Many feel that the expansion of the concept of the book brings "knowledge industries" to a new level of technological sophistication, and that this will have a positive impact on access to knowledge products of all kinds. The expansion of the book certainly is expanding the sophistication of the means of delivering knowledge and entertainment. Encyclopedias issued on CD ROM, for example, have multimedia capability that permit the "reader" to have a different experience than was possible with the traditional printed version. At the same time, the price of such electronic encyclopedias has dropped, although some of the costs for producing such multimedia products have risen. These innovations may, however, have negative implications for those without access to the new technologies or without the resources to produce expensive multimedia products.

It is likely that we will see diversification and differentiation as well as economic concentration in the publishing industry. The impact of the multinational multimedia corporations will continue, and there is likely to be increasing concentration of ownership internationally. Economic realities, the high cost of producing media products, and the impact of the WTO and other trade agreements all point in the direction of concentration. At the same time, there is scope for smaller locally owned firms that can occupy niche markets. In this way, indigenous publishing will be able to survive in an increasingly difficult marketplace.

Publishers face an increasingly complex and competitive environment. They are forced to lower their costs. Editing, for example, is often done on a freelance basis, and publishers in some cases are unable to provide the editorial services once considered standard. More and more of the responsibility for book production has devolved upon the author. Computer composition makes this possible, as authors are often asked to produce their books ready for printing.

The book is secure in the changing economy of knowledge production in the early twenty-first century. Along with the traditional book, however, will be a variety of products based on the book but utilizing the new technologies for presentation as well as for production and distribution.

Conclusion

Publishing, because it is absolutely essential to the cultural, scientific and educational life of nations, has an importance beyond its limited economic role. While it may be appropriate to import textiles or even computers, the production of books that directly reflect the culture, history, and concerns of a nation or people is something that cannot be left to others. Societies cannot afford to lose the ability to publish books of social and cultural importance. It is a vital part of a culture and deserves special consideration.

Book publishing is a small but complex industry. It faces significant challenges from changing patterns of ownership, from changing markets, and from the implications of new technologies. Some have argued that the book will become obsolete in an era dominated by computers and the Internet. This is unlikely. Books are simply too convenient and too affordable. Books permit easy access to information. And in many parts of the world, there is little or no access to the new means of communication. The book as a cultural icon and as a knowledge product is here to stay.

Note

[1] Although Gutenberg is generally credited with the invention of movable type, which made modern printing possible, in fact movable type first appeared in China around 1100 A.D., three centuries prior to Gutenberg, and it appeared in Korea a half century before it was invented in Europe. There seems to be no relationship between these inventions.

Further Reading

Altbach, Philip G., ed., *Copyright and Development: Inequality in the Information Age* (Chestnut Hill, Mass.: Bellagio Publishing Network, 1995).

Altbach, Philip G., ed., *Publishing in Africa and the Third World* (Chestnut Hill, Mass.: Bellagio Publishing Network, 1993).

Altbach, Philip G., ed., *Publishing and Development in the Third World* (London: Hans Zell Publishers, 1992).

Altbach, Philip G., and Hyaeweol Choi, *Bibliography on Publishing and Book Development in the Third World, 1980–1993* (Norwood, N.J.: Ablex, 1993).

Altbach, Philip G., and Edith S. Hoshino, eds., *International Book Publishing: An Encyclopedia* (New York, Garland, 1995).

Barker, Robert, and R. Escarpit, eds., *The Book Hunger* (Paris: UNESCO, 1973).

Chakava, Henry, *Publishing in Africa: One Man's Perspective* (Nairobi, Kenya: East African Educational Publishers, 1996).

Dorsch, P. E., and K. H. Teckentrup, eds., *Buch und Lesen International* (Gütersloh, Germany: Verlag für Buchmarkt und Medien Forschung, 1981).

Estivals, Robert, ed., *Les sciences de l'écrit: Encyclopédie internationale de bibliogie* (Paris: Retz, 1993).

Graham, Gordon, *As I Was Saying: Essays on the International Book Business* (London: Hans Zell Publishers, 1994).

Horowitz, Irving Louis, *Communicating Ideas: The Politics of Scholarly Publishing* (New Brunswick, N.J.: Transaction Publishers, 1991).

Kumar, Narendra, and S. K. Ghai, eds., *Afro-Asian Publishing: Contemporary Trends* (New Delhi: Institute of Book Publishing, 1992).

Ploman, Edward W., and L. Clark Hamilton, *Copyright: Intellectual Property in the Information Age* (London: Routledge & Kegan Paul, 1980).

Smith, Datus C., Jr., *A Guide to Book Publishing* (Seattle: University of Washington Press, 1989).

Taubert, S., and P. Weidhaas, eds., *The Book Trade of the World* (3 vols.) (Munich: K. G. Saur, 1981).

Zell, Hans M., and Cécile Lomer, *Publishing and Book Development in Sub-Saharan Africa: An Annotated Bibliography* (London: Hans Zell Publishers, 1996).

2

Multinationals and Third World Publishing

Gordon Graham

The emergence of multinational media corporations has transformed the structure of the major book publishing industries of Europe and North America in the second half of the twentieth century. Before World War II book publishing companies were small, nationally based and mostly personally owned. By 1990 more than half of all book publishing in Europe and America was controlled by companies that were large, publicly owned, and international. This transformation is irreversible, at least in the short term, if only for the reason that it makes financial sense.

The concentration of independent publishing houses into large groups was not a spontaneous movement. It was engineered by two outside forces. The first, responding to the proliferation of information beyond the capacity that the printed word could efficiently handle, was the revolution in information technology. This revolution was believed in the 1960s to be a threat to the survival of the book and other forms of the printed word. But those engaged in the development of the new technology—of which the computer, the satellite, and the visual display terminal were the three pillars—found that the databanks that they needed to complete their packages, as well as knowledge of the markets and the goodwill of the customers—especially libraries and professional readers—lay in the hands of traditional folio publishers. This led to the initial wave of mergers that took place in the United States in the 1960s as large electronic corporations—ITT, Xerox, CBS, ABC, and Raytheon, for instance—scrambled to acquire book publishing houses.

This scramble engaged a second outside force: the stock market. Old-line publishers were surprised to be approached by brokers and buyers with offers of acquisition at prices that the publishers knew were greater than their companies' intrinsic values. Net physical assets of publishing houses—inventory, receivables, and real estate—became subordinate to the high values set on goodwill and copyright. As a result, many publishing houses were sold, both because they were attracted to substantial capital gains, and because they were daunted by the threat that the burgeoning communications industry, if they resisted takeover, would force them into areas of investment beyond their means. Under pressure from the electronic invaders, publishing houses also began to merge with one another—partly as a defensive move, but partly also in the belief that the developing information society would charge admission prices that only large organizations could afford.

There was also a widespread presumption among both buyers and sellers that the book would progressively decline as the major vehicle for the communication of knowledge, learning, information, and entertainment. This presumption turned out to be wrong in two ways. First, the book continued to unexpectedly prosper, especially in the hands of traditional publishers who refrained from straying into the alien environment of the computer world. Second, the presumed synergy between books and electronic media turned out to be a myth. As a result of the latter, the new media acquisitionors of the 1960s became disenchanted, and divested their acquisitions—often back into the hands of traditional publishing groups that had grown bigger in the interim. It cannot be said, however, that the financial and technical minds who had banked on parleying publishing from its cottage/personal ethos into big business were proved wrong. They were right, but the parleying was done by those who were already in the business.

The fallacious thinking behind the financial synergies is well illustrated by the abortive bid by American Express to take over McGraw-Hill in 1979. McGraw-Hill, a diversified publishing corporation with its roots in the nineteenth century, had been building itself both by acquisition and organic growth during the 1960s and 1970s. While growing substantially, it also remained carefully selective and integrated, and was successful in repelling the American Express bid. McGraw-Hill is today a leading example of a multinational publishing corporation that, from a strong base of the printed word, has embraced electronic modes. Times-Mirror is another example of an American publishing company that has grown into a successful media corporation. Starting from its newspaper base in the 1960s, it acquired a number of carefully harmonized publishing imprints and became durable and prosperous.

All of the successful and large corporate book divisions in the United States today can trace their provenance to personal publishing—often preserved by the names of the imprints they have embraced. The book has not often prospered in a conglomerate environment. While it has proved to be a natural partner with newspapers and magazines, there is little synergy at the operating level as newspapers and magazines depend on advertising revenue. But there is the basic shared ethos of the printed word.

By the 1980s, the process of concentration was accelerated by numerous corporate marriages between publishing and the film and video industry. Examples include Warner, which merged with Time; Paramount, which merged with Simon & Schuster; and General Cinema, which bought Harcourt Brace Jovanovich after the latter was driven close to bankruptcy by a takeover bid from Maxwell Communications, whose disintegration was due in part to an overweening belief in synergies that did not exist or could not be demonstrated.

The 1980s were also marked by a retreat from conglomeracy. The United Kingdom's Reed International sold its paper, paint, and packaging interests in the course of a deliberate strategic plan to turn itself into a purely publishing corporation. Thomson International got out of the oil business and is today solely in magazines, newspapers, and books, except for holiday travel. The fifteen $1 billion plus multinationals that are substantially in the book business, with a total turnover of about $60 billion, see themselves as being in the information, education, and entertainment business. Each uses whatever format or vehicle is most appropriate.

In Europe, the process of mergers and acquisitions leading to the formation of multinational corporations did not take off until the 1970s. Publishing in Europe is compartmentalized by language and culture. Television and radio are mainly state-owned, so there was no parallel movement into publishing comparable with that of the American networks—CBS, NBC, and ABC—in the 1960s. When the mergers did begin, they were stimulated in the United Kingdom by the inroads of certain American corporations, such as Collier Macmillan, and in Europe by the need to break across language barriers in order to expand. Both of these developments stimulated transatlantic acquisitions by European companies. Today, Bertelsmann, Hachette, Elsevier, and Wolters Kluwer from mainland Europe, and Reed and Pearson from the United Kingdom, all have substantial American interests, mostly gotten through acquisitions.

The thirty-year process of concentrating publishing interests from 1960 to 1990 was initially a national phenomenon. It became international because of the common ownership of the English language in Britain and the United States, and the expansion into the English language by the continentals. British and American publishers had long intertraded with each other and had become each other's largest customers, both for the sale of physical books and the purchase of territorial rights. Their arrangements over the latter, known as the Traditional Markets Agreement, came under fire from the United States Justice Department in 1976. Prompted, it was widely believed, by Australian booksellers who had to await the British editions of American bestsellers, the department accused a group of American publishers, with the British Publishers Association as a coconspirator, of breaching antitrust regulations. The settlement of this suit by a consent decree, followed in the 1980s by the emergence of the single market in Europe, not only encouraged some of the larger American trade publishers to retain world rights of the books they published, but also quickened their interest in acquiring British houses. "Vertical integration"—hardcover and paperback editions under the same ownership—was another trend of the 1980s. All of these developments favored larger publishing units, which could become multinational.

Westward Atlantic acquisitions were impelled also by the desire of the Europeans to establish themselves in the largest English-language market. Pearson, a British corporation, acquired Viking and married it with their Penguin imprint in the United States. News Corporation's Harper-Collins was another British initiative. So was Reed International's acquisition of R. R. Bowker. Pearson later acquired Addison-Wesley, and the Thomson Group acquired a whole string of academic and professional houses, after which it transferred its headquarters from the United Kingdom to Canada. Germany's Bertelsmann acquired Bantam-Doubleday-Dell, and France's Hachette acquired Grolier. All of this amounted to a substantial European stake in American publishing.

In the eastern direction, Paramount's Simon & Schuster established a branch in the United Kingdom, and Bantam—by this time a German-owned American house—launched itself as a hardcover publisher in the United Kingdom. So did Newhouse's Random House, by purchasing a group of venerable British imprints. The major American academic houses had already been established in Britain for about twenty years. Thus, by the end of the 1980s, almost every branch of book publishing, with the exception of school textbooks, had become transatlantic, and a small number of large corporations could properly describe themselves as multinational.

"Multinational," however, is not a term that the multinationals use very much. They prefer terms like "global" or "international" in self-descriptions. "Multinational" is, however, an accurate definition of companies with divisions that operate as equal partners in two or more countries, and long predates both its own coinage and the formation of these transatlantic corporations. For example, the leading British houses of the first half of the century—Collins, Macmillan, Longman, Oxford University Press, Butterworths, and others—which established branch houses in Canada, Australia, New Zealand, India, and South Africa primarily as sales agencies but progressively as regional publishers, were an earlier version of publishing multinationals. With the ending of empire, these "overseas branches" continued, where permitted by the postcolonial governments, to conduct their business, especially in the lucrative school book and English-language teaching markets. These activities, which often preferred the adaptation of British books over the generation of local manuscripts, aroused political and commercial opposition, and still do. The postcolonial "cultural imperialism" has lent a pejorative overtone to the word "multinational" in the developing world.

Another form of multinational publishing, predating by about twenty years the emergence of the large transatlantic corporations, was developed by the scientific, technical, and medical (STM) publishers. Houses such as Germany's Springer or the Netherlands' Elsevier, which had had to rebuild themselves from scratch after World War II, were among the first to establish bases either in Britain or the United States or both. An intrinsically transnational field, the thrust of STM publishing in the 1950s and 1960s was aided by the virtuosity of refugee European publishers such as Pergamon's Robert Maxwell, Interscience's Maurits Dekker, and Blackwell Scientific's Per Saugman. While some of the most ambitious publishers originated in Europe, the bulk of the postwar scientific research was being done in the United States. The activities of publishers from and in mainland Europe in due course galvanized the British competitors out of their preoccupation with the old imperial markets and the Americans out of their absorption in their vast home market.

The explosion of research in science, technology, and medicine in the cold war years gave birth to a corpus of literature that was both huge and transnational. While some of it was undertaken by university presses in the United States, and by professional societies on both sides of the Atlantic, this explosion created a number of specialized multinational publishers. Some of the latter were absorbed into the larger corporations created in the 1970s and 1980s, while others, such as Springer or John Wiley, retained their identity and independence into the 1990s. If we ignore the colonial phenomenon as the product of an earlier age, the scientific monograph and journal were arguably the pioneering influences in publishing multinationalism.

Another influence was the American college textbook. In the 1950s the leading college textbook publishers in the United States, such as McGraw-Hill, Prentice Hall, or Addison-Wesley, discovered an enormous export market that had not existed before World War II. This led these companies to establish distribution branches—at first only in the English-speaking world, but later in Europe, Asia, and Latin America. By the 1960s these companies were not only distributing American books, but also publishing locally. While Prentice Hall was acquired by Simon & Schuster and Addison-Wesley by Pearson, McGraw-Hill remains a large multinational with companies in many countries, built mainly by organic growth.

Semantically, there is no reason why a multinational company should not be small and specialized, but the term has come to be identified with scale. The concept includes an assumption of sufficient financial resources to enable entry into foreign countries, whether by acquisition or start-up. The inclusion of the element of size in the definition of multinational results in a list of fewer than twenty publishing corporations that today dominates the industry worldwide. Most of them are in magazines, newspapers, television, and radio, as well as books and journals, and prefer to call themselves communications or information corporations. There are also some very large communications corporations—for example, Reuters—that do not engage in book publishing and others that, while engaged substantially in book publishing—such as Japan's Kodansha or Italy's Mondadori, confine their activities largely to their own countries and cannot be considered as multinationals.

However, the sum of these corporations does not add up to a truly global business. They are largely the outcome of organic growth in and mutual colonization between Europe and North America. While they are regarded with suspicion—occasionally verging on dislike— by those who see them as profit-obsessed behemoths—including those authors, librarians, and booksellers who believe that the book is the province of the creative individualist, their power and influence are widely admired, not least by their shareholders. Although they form a cohesive category, they have little in common with one another except the factors that make them multinationals. Differences of style and culture are profound, and the competition among them is intense.

The one situation in which multinational publishers are bitterly resented is when they move into countries where the local publishing industry is struggling for viability. The multinationals are then accused of stifling the development of a genuinely national literature. Then the indigenous publishers form alliances with the trade and cultural ministries of their governments to contain or repel the invaders. Canada, which has legislated against foreign ownership of publishing houses and has subsidized Canadian-owned houses, is the best example of this phenomenon. The same syndrome can be found in Mexico, where Spain-based publishers are seen as unduly dominant, and in African countries where the British and French multinationals are seen as using their expertise and financial strength to obtain contracts over the heads of the local publishers.

The thirty-year growth of the multinationals from 1960 to 1990 has had a more positive outcome on the welfare of the book than was feared by those who foresaw that creativity and flair would be overshadowed by financial criteria. Book publishing often provides a multinational corporation with a useful element of constancy to offset the volatility of magazines and newspapers and television, which depend for their major income on advertising revenue. This applies particularly to book publishing for professional markets, especially those involving variants of the book such as learned journals, directories, encyclopedias, looseleaf services, and reference books, all of which provide attractive cash flow and lend themselves readily to conversion into databases. Those corporations that have displayed patience and forbearance toward the book have come to appreciate it. Those looking for fast financial returns have sometimes become disenchanted, and resold imprints that they had acquired. Such retreats are often made by television-oriented corporations. For example, CBS sold the Holt, Rinehart and Saunders lists and Time Life sold Scott, Foresman, purchases that they had made expensively and with great hopes. Although the proportion of book publishing in a multinational varies, it is seldom the center of a corporate portfolio. News International is mainly a newspaper business. Reed Elsevier is mainly a magazine and journal business. Paramount, Time Warner, and Harcourt General are mainly film companies. Books form only 23 percent of Sweden's Bonnier; less than 20 percent of News Corporation; about 40 percent of Pearson; and about 20 percent of Reed International and Times-Mirror.

Very few of the world's leading multinational publishing corporations are conglomerates. Their activities, whatever the media they use, are exclusively devoted to information, communications, entertainment, and education. Several have shed some or all of their nonpublishing activities. Of the fifteen leading corporations only Harcourt General (specialty retailing and insurance); Thomson (leisure travel); and Pearson (oil, banking, and fine bone china) have nonpublishing divisions. It is probable that the book alone is not a broad enough base to support a corporation with a turnover in excess of $1 billion. Harcourt Brace is one example of a corporation that attempted this, and, after great difficulty in defending itself against the bid from Maxwell Communications, had to sell to a conglomerate.

It is probable that there is an optimum size for a freestanding multinational devoted entirely to books, but no one knows what this size is. There is a considerable gap between the large multinationals and those book publishing enterprises consisting of clusters of imprints, formed defensively during the waves of mergers and acquisitions. While the book has shown unexpected strength in the face of the electronic challenge, it is quite possible that its growth rate is compared unfavorably with that of the electronic media by corporate managements. The counteranswer to this would have to be innovation—the starting of new lists. Most of the lists acquired by the corporations serve mature markets, where the growth rate is inevitably slower.

Meanwhile, the fastest rate of growth within book publishing in the 1990s is not in the corporations or groups but in new independent companies, many of them very small. Self-publishing, aided by desktop equipment, is becoming more common. Book publishing is a business of constant self-renewal, each new title being a separate microventure. That is why it does not always prosper under centralized or large-scale systematized management. As divisions of large corporations, book publishing appears to prosper best with maximum decentralization, using editors who know how to build lists and win authors, and publishers who are content with the book as their chosen vehicle and do not see it merely as a sector within the information industry.

At the same time, there are national limitations in many book publishing programs. The transnationalism that corporations can bring—for example, through intertrading among sister companies in many countries—should give the book scope that the small independent publisher cannot achieve. Production and distribution are other areas where corporate management and financial discipline can be of benefit. Using production facilities throughout the world, and installing sophisticated and expensive computer facilities are things that corporations do well. The availability of funds for major investments, albeit with stringent financial checks, is another corporate benefit for book publishing. Corporations should also be able to gain experience through their acquisitions of different kinds of lists, which can be transferred from one division to another, and from one country to another.

It is significant that corporations, on becoming multinational, acquire a common vocabulary. The following mission statements are quoted from the annual reports of five of the world's leading corporations from five different countries—France, Germany, the Netherlands, Britain, and the United States. It would be difficult to guess the nationalities of the corporations from these statements:

- "We are dedicated to helping people share knowledge and have access to a comprehensive range of information, news and events."
- "Our operations in thirty-eight countries span the creation, production and distribution of books, newspapers and magazines, radio, TV and film products, and advertising display."
- "We are in the business of news and entertainment. We are committed to the generation and dissemination of information and ideas."
- "We provide information in print through books, magazines and newsletters; on-line or with electronic networks; over the air by television and satellite; and on software, video tape, facsimile and compact discs."
- "As the world leader in media and entertainment, we take it as our responsibility to lead in ways that go beyond the bottom line—whether in fighting for a healthier society, improving the education of our children, wiping out functional illiteracy, or opening up the marketplace of ideas to the widest diversity of human thought and experience."

While the border-leaping electronic imperative has been a major propulsion of the multinational phenomenon, the unacknowledged tide that has carried the corporations into many lands is the speed with which the English language has increased its dominance as the world's main commercial language. Those corporations that have grown dramatically are either based in countries where English is the native language, or have taken deliberate decisions to move out of their own language cultures. Those corporations that have not moved out of their native languages, such as Bonnier (Sweden), Mondadori (Italy), Anaya (Spain), or Kodansha (Japan) have either been contained, or have chosen to remain within the parameters of their national cultures, which can make excellent sense in terms of profits, but is bound to slow down top-line growth in the end.

But the English language does not mean the whole world. All of the leading corporations employ self-descriptions such as globalism or world leadership, but their vision is limited by their commercial judgment, by the vagaries of international politics, by exchange fluctuations and by the way that each nation favors its own. The total world stage, including Asia, the Middle East, Africa, and Latin America does not offer an even platform for short-term expansion. It is much easier to take root in a mature economy by purchasing parts of an established industry than to venture into an immature economy. The great corporations have rarely ventured into the developing economies or into the struggling postcommunist economies of Eastern Europe and Russia. The expatriate pioneers in such territories are more often specialist companies. For example, Yale University Press has a joint venture with a group of publishers in Shanghai on the history of Chinese art. Readers Digest has started a Russian edition. The uncertainty of copyright is another deterrent. As a result, there is little rapport between the developing economies, where capital investment in publishing is most needed, and the multinationals, which have the capital to invest but are governed by their self-set standards of return on investment.

Multinationals are accustomed to, and prefer, a minimum of state interference. They have battened on the progressive deregulation in the developed world and are not comfortable with bureaucracies. Building an enterprise in countries such as India or Kenya or Egypt when one is not a national, calls for reserves of patience and agility and cultural sensitivity that are more likely to be found in individual entrepreneurs than in large organizations. It is therefore likely that the multinationals will continue to confine themselves to the developed economies, and will experience a slower growth rate in the next three decades than in the last. Investment of corporate resources will be directed toward market share and innovation rather than to shaky economies with soft currencies. The movements that created the multinationals—the information revolution, the English language, and economic deregulation—carry in the end their own limits. The absence of any serious publishing multinational presence in the booming economies of Asia is a significant pointer to the limits that the multinationals have set for themselves. Some have outposts in places such as Singapore, Hong Kong, or Japan, but no roots, and little multinationalism exists in countries where Chinese is more likely to be spoken than English.

In estimating the future growth of the multinationals, distinction must also be made between those parts of their business that are national and those that are transnational. School publishing or law publishing or regional newspapers, for example, are all national industries by definition and can grow no faster than the economies of the countries in which they are located. Other subjects are by definition transnational, such as travel or finance or science. It is in these areas that most multinationals probably see their future growth, since they offer power bases, identifiable professional constituencies, and easy translation into the electronic mode—all on a scale with which the purely national publisher is ill-equipped to compete.

Book publishing, although there is talk of globalism, remains mainly a national business, relating to the culture of each country. Very few book titles have a genuinely worldwide appeal. There is little overlap between the bestseller lists of the major publishing countries. STM books and journals are an exception. It is not surprising that they are popular with multinationals and that they are the only genre in book publishing to have their own international organization—the STM Group, founded in Amsterdam in 1968.

When analyzed, most of the book publishing done by multinationals emerges as an assembly of book publishing houses rather than a single large house. When such an assembly is cumulatively profitable, this is due more to the fact that the component houses are individually profitable than because they are of material help to one another. Only in a financial sense can weaker lists be sheltered under stronger. In the end, each list has to prove itself. Operating economies can sometimes be demonstrated when two similar companies merge and combine their premises or services. But this is a one-off savings. Economies claimed for scale per se are few in the book business. For example, sales and profits can be enhanced when companies in different countries with common ownership trade with one another. While the electronic modes become more efficient and profitable as they get bigger, the book remains stubbornly individual, and for that reason will remain more of a passenger than a driver on the multinational vehicle. But a very welcome passenger.

A question that the Euro-American multinationals will face in the twenty-first century is how to collaborate or compete or associate with what will then be the large and prosperous publishing industries of Asia, and in due course of the Middle East, Africa, and Latin America. Each corporation will decide for itself to what extent it embraces these larger continents in its long-term strategy. Although the communications industry is one of the largest and by far the most influential in the world, it has no overall sense of identity. It makes no sense, therefore, for the outsider to refer to "the multinationals," as if they were a power group. The fifteen or twenty largest corporations with book publishing elements are located in seven countries on both sides of the Atlantic. Some of them are owned or controlled by single individuals or families. Some are publicly owned and responsible to thousands of shareholders. While all have public consciences and goals, these are circumscribed by their fiduciary duties to be financially prudent. Boardroom decisions are taken always with a watchful eye on the trading value of a company's shares, and there is no reason why those in the communications business should differ in this respect from those in oil, transport, or pharmaceuticals. Nevertheless, all of the corporations display an awareness that the merchandise in which they deal has a unique potential for good or ill, as the messages in their annual reports never fail to state.

In a century marked in general by decline in respect for and influence of the traditional institutions—government, church, law, and/or the family—the communications industry has gained power and influence and has become identified in the public mind, if not in its own, as a neoinstitution called "the media." The multinationals are thus thrust into a position of responsibility to which their response is uneven. That which has mainly contributed to their growth—the electronic revolution and the world-homogenizing effect of this revolution—emphasizes mass communication through which it is hard to satisfy individual tastes and styles. Newspapers and news magazines are published simultaneously in a dozen cities around the world. Cable television broadcasts news, and frequently influences news, twenty-four hours a day in all the world's time zones. Researchers with personal computers can tap into international networks. To all of this the book, the oldest vehicle of communication, is a necessary counterbalance.

Meanwhile the nascent publishing industries of the developing world and the reformed industries of the postcommunist world are growing in a more traditional way. While multinationals, seeing no short-term scope in line with their financial goals, corral themselves in the mature markets, publishing industries at a earlier stage of development grow as expressions of national culture and language, and at such stages, the book is the ideal vehicle. These industries, relying on print and paper to serve the four-fifths of the world's population outside of Western Europe and North America, could become in the next decade or two a force comparable to, or larger than, that of today's multinational communications industry.

It is an industry not strong in philosophic direction. It grew for commercial reasons, through mergers and acquisitions, into a transatlantic business rooted mainly in the English language. Almost one-fifth of the United States book business fell, or leapt, into the hands of non-American firms between 1960 and 1990. American corporations responded by preemptive bids for colleague companies in the United States and by activating a hitherto mild interest in the ownership of companies in Britain. By the end of the 1980s there were few new businesses, but the old ones had been grouped and reoriented. This was not done from any vision of globalism. Globalism was invented to justify the jockeying for position among large competitors who, for whatever reasons, had outgrown the scope within their national boundaries. The westward thrust from Europe has been the principal catalyst. The European incursions into the United States encouraged American managements to take a longer view. The survival, indeed prosperity, of the book took the European houses less by surprise than the Americans, because the former were steeped historically in the ethos of the book and the latter were often neopublishers drawn into the book business. Encouraged by a favorable exchange rate with the dollar and a degree of deregulation that promised the possibility of market leadership in a market not divided by language and culture, the Europeans established a major presence in the United States. Closer geographically to Eastern Europe, closer philosophically, through their colonial history, to the concept of multinationalism, and now themselves in economic union, the Europeans will probably be the ones to extend publishing multinationalism most vigorously into the other continents.

3

The Economics of Book Publishing

Datus C. Smith, Jr.

The book publisher is an investor in books. The publisher is the one who pays out money to the author, translator, artist, editor, printer, papermaker, and others for producing the books, and to the salespeople, advertisers, and those who help in marketing them, and takes in money from booksellers and others who buy the books or who buy the right to use the books' content in some way. The publisher hopes to take in more money than is paid out.

That is the whole story of "the economics of book publishing." Everything else here, and in the millions of words in many languages written on the subject through the years, is only a refinement of that basic theme.

As in any business, the book publisher tries to reduce costs and increase income but realizes that "you have to spend money to make money." It is the purpose of this chapter to look at some of the relationships of cost to income and final profit.

The surest way to increase income is to sell more books. More income should increase profit, if the publisher is a commercial house, or reduce the need for subsidy, if the publisher is a nonprofit organization. That is a more profound statement than appears at first glance, for it rests on a fundamental principle of book publishing: manufacturing *costs per copy* go down not just a little bit but often sensationally as the quantity increases. As we shall see in a moment, that is dramatically true for manufacturing costs, but it is also true in greater or less degree for many other of the publisher's expenses.

The successful publisher is the one who recognizes that principle, and learns how to make use of it. That is what makes the difference between a vigorous and expanding and profitable book publishing industry and one that plods along with the same old high prices, low sales, and low profits—and, incidentally, small contribution to the national welfare.

Cost

There are two ways of looking at the items of the book publisher's cost. The first way considers merely what is done in the various operations, and the costs fall into three main groups:

Editorial preparation costs. This category includes the publisher's payment to the author and salaries or fees to the illustrator, editor, translator (if the book is to be a translation rather than an original work), designer, and others.

Physical manufacturing costs. This includes payment to the printer for printing the books and (either directly or through the printer) to the manufacturers of paper, ink, cloth, thread, glue, and so forth.

Marketing and distribution costs. Included here is the work of sales representatives, order clerks, shippers, advertisers, promoters, and others.

That is a perfectly logical way of looking at costs, and for some purposes it is the best way. But there is a more useful method for analysis of how the factors can influence the cost of a book and, eventually, the size of the publisher's profit.

This second method of studying costs is the one a farseeing publisher uses when deciding how many copies of a book should be printed, what selling price to charge, how far to go in meeting an author's demand for a higher rate of royalty payment, and so forth. Under this other method of listing the kinds of expense, they are divided into groups showing how their size is influenced by the number of copies:

Automatically varying costs. These are costs that automatically increase for a given book if the number of copies is increased.

1. Royalty payments to the author, usually based on number of copies sold; sometimes a flat amount based on the size of the edition printed.
2. Payments to the printer for presswork and binding (this does *not* include the cost of composition, which is an unvarying cost in the category below).
3. Payment for materials, through the printer or directly to the supplier of paper, ink, cloth, thread, staples, glue, and so forth.
4. Storage and shipping.

Unvarying costs. These are costs that do not vary for a given book, whatever the number of copies printed.

1. Editorial preparation, including editing, illustration, cover design, and so forth.

2. Composition, that is, the typesetting, calligraphing, and plate-making—in other words the preparatory stage of bookmaking up to the point when the press starts putting ink on paper.

Promotion costs. These vary according to the publisher's policy decision, naturally influenced by the number of copies but not automatically following it.

Overhead costs. These can be controlled by the publisher to some extent in view of expectation of sales for all the books published, but in general are fixed costs: administration, accounting, taxes, rent, interest on borrowed capital, and so forth.

The following comments provide one example from each expense category to help make the distinction clear.

AUTOMATICALLY VARYING COSTS

Paper is a clear case of an expense that goes up or down almost directly in proportion to the number of copies. There are ten times as many kilograms of paper in an edition of 10,000 books as in one of 1,000. And although there is some variation in the price per kilogram depending on whether a little or a lot is bought at one time, one may say in general that the cost of paper is in direct proportion to the number of copies.

UNVARYING COSTS

On the other hand, typesetting is a good example of a cost that is the same for a given book whatever the number of copies. When the compositors set the type, their job is no more difficult, and the cost no greater, whether one copy is to be printed or a million. And because the *total* typesetting cost is unchanged, the cost *per copy* of course goes down as the quantity increases. For instance, if it costs §1,000[1] to set type for a book that is to be printed in an edition of 1,000 copies, the typesetting will be §1 *per copy;* or if an edition of 10,000 copies, then the typesetting cost goes down to §0.1 *per copy;* and so on.

PROMOTION COSTS

Advertising is an item of expense for which the publisher's policy judgment will be *influenced by* the number of copies, but there is nothing automatic about it. Many publishers plan on spending a fixed percentage of the year's sales income on advertising, and they use that figure for overall estimating. But the expenditure for any particular book is decided in the light of many factors, including the kind of book as well as the quantity the publisher thinks can be sold, how the public is expected to respond to different kinds of advertising, and so forth.

OVERHEAD COSTS

It is clear that most such costs are relatively fixed and, in the short term, cannot be changed very much, or at least not with respect to any one book. Although the publisher may engage or discharge administrative staff or accountants and thus make some adjustment for increases or decreases in the overall business, it is not possible to cut off and sell half the office or warehouse or delivery truck if business suddenly declines by 50 percent. It is in this sense that we call these costs fixed.

The publisher wants to include, in the price purchasers are asked to pay for the book, a sufficient allowance for overhead cost. It is never possible to calculate exactly what should be charged to each book, but the year's total overhead expense to be charged to *all* of the publisher's books can be estimated; and then it can be assigned to individual books in various ways. A common method is to assume the overhead cost in the future will be about the same percentage of net sales income as it was in the previous year. If last year's sales totaled §400,000 and overhead costs totaled §100,000, the publisher assumes that the overhead in the coming year will probably again be 25 percent of net sales income. To complete this illustration by applying it in a specific case: if the publisher guessed that there would be §10,000 sales income from a particular book it could be roughly estimated that the overhead cost of that book would be 25 percent of §10,000 or §2,500. The 25 percent figure used here is merely an example; the overhead percentage varies widely from one country to another and from one publisher to another as well.

We will come back to the question of cost when putting the expense figures and income figures together in a later section of this chapter. But first, let us see what determines how much sales income the publisher gets.

Income

The main influences on the amount of sales income are only vaguely imagined by most people outside the book business. The typical layman, upon hearing that a publisher has brought out an edition of 5,000 copies of a book with a selling price of §3 does some quick figuring and decides the publisher has an income of §15,000. How wrong that is! Discussed below are the four major factors a publisher has in mind in calculating possible income.

1. *Selling price.* For reasons we shall study later, the relation of the manufacturing cost of a book to the selling price is quite different in Asia and Africa from what it is in Europe and the United States. Many Asians have a general rule of multiplying the manufacturing cost by only 3 to 3.5 to determine the selling price, whereas in publishing industries in other parts of the world the factor may be 4, 4.5, 5, 6, or even more for certain kinds of books.

2. *Number of copies sold.* This is, of course, the major risk in any book publishing project. If a large part of the edition is unsold, all the calculations are thrown off. But even if the edition is sold out, that will not be the full number of copies because of the free copies given away for promotion and the damaged copies.

3. *Discount to booksellers and other purchasers.* Booksellers always receive a discount from the publisher; jobbers and wholesalers get an additional discount; and other kinds of purchasers get discounts of different kinds and sizes. Although some purchasers pay the full listed price, the average is brought down by the large purchasers with large discounts. In the United States discounts may run as high as 55 percent or more, and the average for many general books can be about 44 percent; in Europe the discount sale tends to be lower and in Asia and Africa very much lower.

4. *Incidental cost of marketing.* These costs include commissions to certain kinds of sales representatives, uncollectable debts from purchasers, postage in those cases where the publisher pays the carrying charge, and so forth. Such costs can run from a very low figure to more than 15 percent.

For the example above of an edition of 5,000 copies of a book selling at §3, let us assume that 100 copies of the book are damaged or given away free, so there are only 4,900 to sell; that average discounts are 25 percent; and that incidental selling costs are 3 percent. We would then get this result:

Selling price of 4,900 copies @ §3	§14,700
Less average 25% discount to purchasers	§ 3,675
Total paid by purchasers	§11,025
Less incidental selling costs, 3% of sales	§ 330
Net sales income for the publisher	§10,695

That is quite different from the §15,000 predicted by the naive person outside the book industry! And this particular example is more favorable to the publisher than the average in most of the world's book industries because of the low average discount we have assumed.

Cost versus Income

Thus far we have been considering cost and income separately. The real test of publishing wisdom comes when you try to fit the two together. You would like to charge more for the book, but the higher selling price might decrease the number of sales; you would like to encourage booksellers by allowing more discount, but that would reduce the sales income per copy sold; you would like to use cheaper paper, but the less attractive book may be so much less appealing to the public that your loss of sales may be greater than your saving of expense.

There is a never-ending series of such relationships for all books, as well as surprises in the performance of particular books. The genius of book publishing lies in the vision and analytical intelligence with which the publisher sees how to increase quantities, reduce prices, and get more profit, all at the same time.

As suggested earlier, the most important key to achieving this is the principle of how per copy costs decline as quantities increase. The saving in per copy costs when quantities increase is not, at present, as great in Asia and Africa as it is in Europe and the United States and, to some extent, in Latin America because (1) the developing countries do not yet have enough equipment giving the full saving for long press runs compared with short ones, and (2) in view of the high cost of paper and the relatively low cost of labor in most Asian and African countries, paper cost (which we have seen does not vary much per copy) is a larger element in the cost of a book than printing cost (which *does* become less per copy with increasing quantities) in countries with more developed book industries.

Even so, in every country on earth the important fact to note at all times is: *per copy costs go down as quantities go up*. See how the principle works out in the example in Table 1—an imaginary one based on actual figures from a combination of Asian, African, and Latin American countries. The actual figures would not be right in any one country because of differences in printing and paper costs, in publishing practices, in discount schedules, and so forth, and especially in the completeness with which the publisher does the job and bears the cost of his full publishing responsibility. But the example illustrates the basic fact.

Table 1. Cost of Producing Books

	1,000-copy edition	5,000-copy edition	10,000-copy edition
Composition (typesetting) cost unaffected by quantity	§237.00*	§237.00	§237.00
Presswork and binding	121.00	400.00	746.00
Paper	103.00	500.00	1,000.00
	§461.00	§1,137.00	§1,983.00
Cost per copy	§0.46	§0.23	§0.20

*§ = a generalized representation of a money unit of any country.

Another way of stating the per copy saving when producing the larger quantity is to say that although the first thousand copies cost §0.46 each, an additional 4,000 copies could be produced at the same time at a cost of only §0.17 each.

The most important element in this critical fact of low *run-on* costs is the decreasing cost *per copy* of composition as the size of the edition increases. Figure 1 shows this.

Figure 1. Composition costs shown as a percentage of total book manufacturing cost.

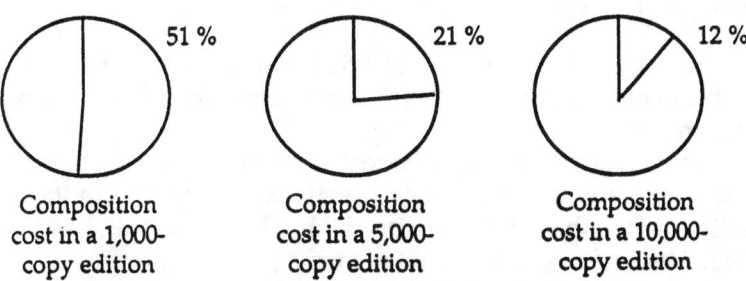

| Composition cost in a 1,000-copy edition | Composition cost in a 5,000-copy edition | Composition cost in a 10,000-copy edition |

Note: Full circles represent the cost of manufacturing one copy in editions of three different sizes. Indicated areas show the varying cost of composition (figures show the composition cost as a percentage of the full manufacturing cost).

Or the facts can be presented in another way, showing directly the low run-on costs of additional copies manufactured at the same time. In the next chart (Figure 2) the three bars show the per copy cost of the book in editions of the three sizes. The costs of composition, presswork, and paper make up the total in each case. As noted above, the composition cost *per copy* goes down greatly as the edition becomes larger. Presswork and paper are the run-on costs.

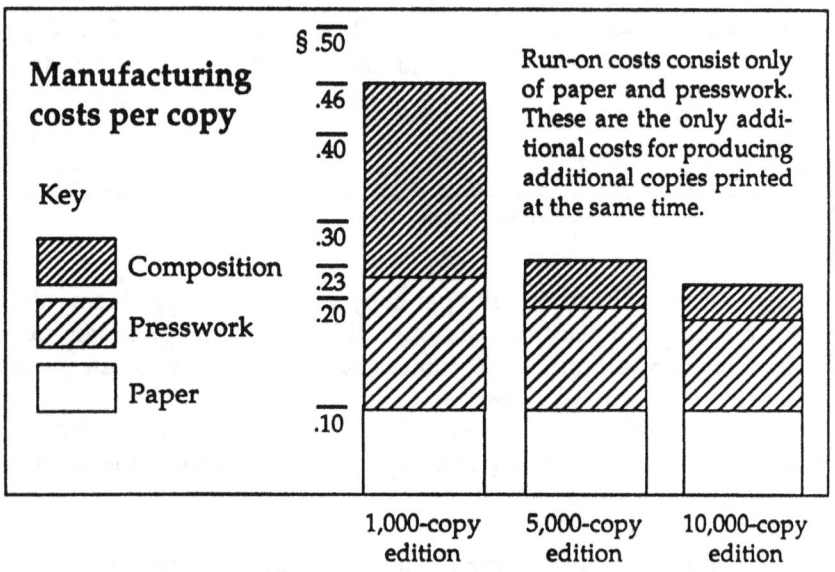

Figure 2. Manufacturing cost of one copy in editions of three different sizes.

Publishing Cost

The cost of production, just discussed, is only one part of the publisher's cost; and of course income has to be calculated to consider the profit or loss on a book.

Because some of the publisher's costs relate directly to the selling price (for instance, the author's royalty is usually a percentage of the selling price), the price at which the book is to be sold has to be decided before doing the rest of the figuring.

In the case of this hypothetical book, we assume the publisher might apply a multiplying factor of something like 3.5 to the per copy manufacturing cost shown in Table 1—that is, that the selling price would be fixed at three and one-half times the per copy manufacturing cost. And we assume that in the country of publication a publisher's average income from sales (after allowing discounts to booksellers, etc.) is about 70 percent of the selling price. And, finally, we assume that the free copies given away for promotion and the damaged copies will reduce the number of copies for sale somewhat below the number printed. These hypotheses are calculated in Table 2.

The publisher's full cost can then be put together as shown in Table 3.

Table 2. Selling Price and Sales Income

	1,000-copy edition	5,000-copy edition	10,000-copy edition
Production cost per copy (see Table 1)	§0.46	§0.23	§0.20
Selling price	§1.50	§0.80	§0.75
Average sales income per copy (70% of selling price)	§1.05	§0.56	§0.53
Number of copies available for sale (after deducting free and damaged copies)	950	4,900	9,850
Total sales income	§998	§2,744	§5,220

Finally, putting together the income from Table 2 and the publishing cost from Table 3, we see the profit situation for the editions of different size (if all copies are sold) in Table 4.

The relationship of cost to profit in editions of different size is of course a key point. Note that: for the 5,000-copy edition the *cost* is 2.5 times the cost of the 1,000-copy edition, but the *profit* would be 7.5 times as great if all copies were sold; for the 10,000-copy edition the cost is about 4.5 times the cost of the 1,000-copy edition, but the *profit* would be nearly 18 times as great if all copies were sold.

If all copies are sold, in other words, the publisher's *profit in relation to the amount risked in paying for production* increases greatly as the size of the edition goes up. The charts in Figure 3 give the picture.

Table 3. Full Publishing Cost

	1,000-copy edition	5,000-copy edition	10,000-copy edition
Selling price	§1.50	§0.80	§0.75
Number copies to sell	950	4,900	9,850
Production cost (from Table 1)	§461	§1,137	§1,983
Author's royalty ((10% of selling price for first 5,000; 12.5% after that)*	142	392	831
Advertising, estimated	100	200	300
Overhead, estimated at 25% of the net sales income shown in Table 2†	250	686	1,305
Full publishing cost	§953	§2,415	§4,418

*The royalty figure here is just an example. There are many different royalty rates, and in recent years there has been a tendency to fix the royalty as a percentage of the publisher's net receipts, rather than of the list price of the book. There are also different rates for paperback editions, for export sales, and so forth.
†The overhead estimate of 25% is also just an example. In many developed book industries a 40% overhead allowance is more usual.

Figure 3. Profit as percentage of production cost.

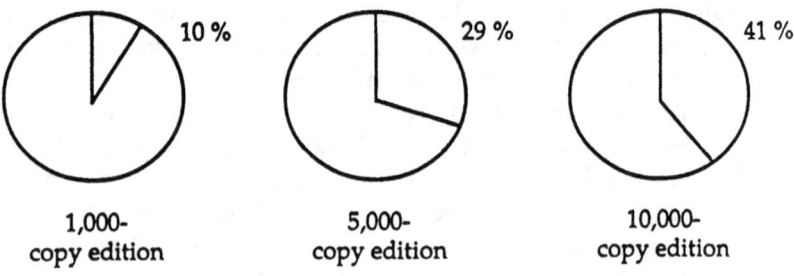

Note: Full circles represent production cost; indicated areas show profit.

Calculating the Break-Even Point

A method of figuring that publishers sometimes use when deciding printing quantities and selling prices is that of calculating what is called the break-even point—that is, the number of copies that will have to be sold in order to recover manufacturing cost. The trouble with the method is that it does not necessarily include correct overhead costs for selling part of an edition; but applications of overhead to particular books are inaccurate in other ways as well, and this break-even approach has value for rough estimating.

Table 4. Possible Profit

	1,000-copy edition	5,000-copy edition	10,000-copy edition
Income from Table 2	§998	§2,744	§5,220
Publishing cost from Table 3	§953	§2,415	§4,418
Profit if all copies sold	§45	§329	§802

The publisher first calculates what margin per copy, after paying other expenses, will be left over for meeting production costs. That margin figure is then divided into the total production cost, thus giving a rough idea of how many copies must be sold before breaking even. Here is an application of the method to the above book in the 5,000-copy edition:

Selling price of the book (5,000-copy edition)	§0.80
Less average discount estimated at 30%	0.24
Net sales income per copy	§0.56
Less (per copy):	
Author's royalty (10% of selling price)	§0.08
Overhead (25% of net sales income)	0.14
Advertising	0.05
	0.27
Margin per copy for paying for production	§0.29

Break-even point: §1,137 ÷ §0.29 = 3,921 copies

Thus if the book is published in a 5,000-copy edition at a selling price of §0.80 and with the other conditions as given, the publisher can recover the manufacturing cost by selling 3,921 copies. The reader may enjoy making a study of the break-even point for the 10,000-copy edition.

Subsidiary Rights

The income discussed in all of the examples above has been entirely from the sale of books. But there is another kind of income to be kept in mind, though it is often of a minor sort in a book industry that is not highly developed: income from the sale or licensing of what are called subsidiary rights, including permission to other publishers to bring out reprint editions; the granting of translation rights; authorization to include excerpts in anthologies or books of readings which other publishers are issuing; and (although this particular income often goes entirely to the author and none to the publisher) authorization to present the work on the stage or on film, radio, television, tape, or videotape.

It should be noted here that there has been a tendency in some developed book industries in recent years, notably that of the United States, for income from subsidiary rights to make a great difference—often the whole difference—between the publisher's profit and loss. That is, many American publishers make a profit of only 2 or 3 percent—or actually sustain a loss—on their regular operations in publishing books, but have a large profit overall because of very substantial income from subsidiary rights.

At present, there is not much income from subsidiary rights for book publishers in Asia, Africa, and Latin America. It can become increasingly important, however, especially as mass distribution schemes are carried out, with a natural increase in cheap reprintings in large quantities of books that may have been issued originally by other publishers. If book publishing in other countries follows the line of development it has taken in Europe and North America, royalty income paid to the original publisher from the mass distribution and book club reprint rights can—at least in theory—become a major source of income. It must be recognized, however, that there has been little progress along this line in the last twenty years. As the West becomes more interested in the literature of developing countries, however, there will be increasing quotation from that literature in anthologies and other possibilities of subsidiary rights, with income for Asian and African and Latin

American publishers from that source.

Economies for the Publisher

There are a thousand ways for the publisher to increase profits besides the basic major way of selling more books. Merely to reduce expenses in the editorial department, in production, in the sales department, and so forth, will not necessarily increase profits, because sales income may be reduced as a result of an unwise economy. Special mention, however, is made in the following section of the two kinds of expense that are indispensable and are related to each other—long-range development and the cost of interest on capital needed if the publisher is going to build for the future.

Capital and Interest

A constant expense in any business is the cost of the capital required—the interest that has to be paid on the money invested in a project from the time the expenses are met until the money comes back in the form of income. Interest is a cost of investment even if the publisher does not have to borrow. Even if the publisher is so lucky as to have plenty of available cash, making it unnecessary to borrow from banks or elsewhere, the capital still costs something because the money could be profitably invested somewhere else, if not in book publishing.

This is perhaps a good place to say that most of the principles in this chapter are as applicable in a socialist as in a capitalist economy, though they are expressed here in terms of a private enterprise system of book publishing. The methods, value judgments, and objectives in the two systems differ in particular circumstances, but an able professional book publisher in either system will look at many of the factors in the same way, and especially the factors of cost.

The question of interest on capital is a case in point: even if, in a state publishing enterprise, the publisher has merely to request an appropriation from the national treasury, that is still part of the national wealth which could be put to good use in some other way if the state did not invest it in book publishing. The conscientious state publisher, as a temporary caretaker of public funds, will regard interest on capital as a true cost of the operation, especially in thinking about long-term investments, whether or not "interest" is an actual entry in the book of account.

To return to the general question of interest on capital as a cost of book publishing, the picture is clearer if we think of interest costs of three sorts: (1) interest cost of normal operations, (2) investment in inventory, and (3) long-term development.

INTEREST COST OF NORMAL OPERATIONS

This category includes advance payments that the publisher may make to the author, and those almost surely to be made to the printer and paper merchant; and the credit to be extended, for at least some period of time, to at least some of the purchasers; and of course the normal running expenses of the publishing house.[2]

INVESTMENT IN INVENTORY

Remembering the inexpensiveness of producing additional copies of a book at the time of first printing, the publisher may think it wise to print more than just a year's supply. For some kinds of books, this can be a wonderful benefit in future years, as steady income is received without further printing cost. But it ties up capital in the meantime, and that cost must be balanced against printing economy. Storage and insurance costs are likewise incurred, as well as the risk of damage from mold and insects. And the high cost of paper in developing countries makes long-term investment less attractive in those areas.

LONG-TERM DEVELOPMENT

This kind of investment, though perhaps bringing no return at all in the year in which the money is spent, can be more important than any other kind for the ultimate good of the individual publisher and of the national book industry of which he is a part. Included in this category are such things as (1) experiments in new distributing methods; (2) long-term projects in editorial development, such as series, new kinds of textbooks, subscription projects, and large reference works; (3) cooperative efforts, with others, in developing more readers and more book purchasers, better schools, additional libraries, and so forth; and (4) projects in industry betterment, such as publishers' associations, trade magazines, a cooperative credit bureau, and exchange of industry information.

The Need for Publisher's Credit

The lack of risk capital, or at least of capital that its owners are willing to invest in the future of their own countries, holds back development in many parts of Asia, Africa, and Latin America. The problem is especially acute in the book publishing industry (though less so in the printing industry, perhaps because the potential investors can see tangible machinery), and undercapitalization is perhaps the most serious single obstacle to book publishing development in the developing countries. This is not merely because the lack of capital forces the publisher to print small quantities at high prices, but because it prevents all the other long-range efforts at building for the future—not only the future economic welfare of the publisher, but also future service to society.

Because book publishing is so small an industry—so small an economic fact in direct terms—in comparison with agriculture, armament-manufacturing plants, and port facilities, the people who draft national financial and economic plans rarely consider the publisher's need for credit. Yet if, for lack of a business loan at a sensible rate of interest, the publisher is forced to go to bazaar moneylenders and pay 25 percent or more, the result is clearly against public welfare. Not only does the publisher have to charge more for books, forcing up the price of textbooks and other basic tools of national education, but in view of that terrible cost of borrowed money, the publisher dare not print more than the minimum number of copies certain to be sold. The publisher is thus prevented from using the principle we studied earlier concerning per copy costs when quantities are increased.

One of the special reasons for cooperation among publishers is to present facts like these to national planners and financial officials, in terms not of the publishers' desires but of national necessity. They need also to enlist the help of others, notably the ministry of education and the intellectual leaders of the country, in giving the public some understanding of how the public welfare is tied up with the economic welfare of this small but critically important industry.

Economic and Public Service

But the publisher has no right to claim public support unless truly serving the public interest, not merely from day to day but also in building for the future in the ways mentioned above. And there are some other ways as well.

A special form of long-term investment is a deliberate decision a publisher sometimes makes to pass on to the consumer through a lower selling price an economy achieved in producing a book, even though, in pure theory, the extra profit could be pocketed. Another form of long-term investment is made sometime or other by every publisher whose sense of financial interest is based on a sense of honor and a concept of public service: the cool decision to go ahead and publish a book that society needs, or that will give a start to a writer of great promise, even though the publisher is pretty sure no money will be made on that particular book.

This talk about the publisher's obligation to society might seem better suited to a philosophical discussion than to this chapter on economics, but in fact it is appropriate here. Most of the truly successful book publishers in the developed book industries of the world have won their most priceless financial asset—the respect and loyalty of authors and booksellers and readers and educators—because they have had so clear a view of the relation between the public interest and their own commercial interest. They have not been unbusinesslike, nor have they turned away from the hard facts of economics. But they know that a firm that is hoping for a long future must think of the consumer at all times and must take risks.

The book publisher, like other people in business, has a kind of license from society to make money in the publication of books. Risk-taking is the fee paid to society for that privilege.

Notes

[1] Throughout this essay we will use the "§" for all money figures, as a generalized representation of a money unit of any country.

[2] Note, by the way, that, to the extent to which the publisher extends credit to purchasers, the publisher is in effect providing them with finance capital; and to the extent to which authors or printers or paper merchants provide their service or material to a publisher without advance payments, they are helping to provide the publisher with finance capital.

4

International Copyright

Paul Gleason

Article 27 of the Universal Declaration of Human Rights, which was adopted by the United Nations General Assembly in 1948, declares:
1. Everyone has the right freely to participate in the culture of the community, to enjoy the arts and to share in scientific advancement and its benefits.
2. Everyone has the right to the protection of the moral and material interests resulting from any scientific, literary or artistic production of which he is the author.

These fundamental and long-established principles have provided the rationale for the enactment and enforcement of copyright laws by nations all over the world. The term "international copyright" is used to describe the collection of bilateral and multilateral agreements among nations to protect literary and artistic works (understood here to include scientific works)—books, films, musical compositions, videotapes, computer software, audio tapes, television programs, sound recordings, and many others—outside their own borders by harmonizing their respective copyright laws. Literary and artistic works are a subdivision of intellectual property (essentially, works that require intellectual effort to create), which also includes industrial property: inventions, trademarks, and industrial designs.

Today's national copyright laws serve several purposes: (1) to guarantee an author a monopoly, or exclusive, right to control the uses made of his or her own (original) work for a specified period; (2) to guarantee a publisher a monopoly right to publish (or arrange to publish) and sell a work within national boundaries for a specified period; (3) to provide financial compensation (royalties) to authors to reward them for their creative work; and (4) to encourage progress in the country's arts and sciences (understood here to encompass the humanities as well as the social sciences) in order to foster its economic, social, and cultural development. Edward Ploman and L. Clark Hamilton observe that "copyright is used as a legal mechanism for the ordering of social and cultural life, or, put another way, copyright is one method for linking the world of ideas to the world of commerce."[1]

National copyright laws have often created, and continue to create, considerable controversy and rancorous disputes among authors, publishers, governments, and larger societies. In particular, the granting of a legal monopoly to publishers—which clearly has helped to provide them with sufficient confidence in their chances of recovering, through sales, their investment in editing, publishing, marketing, and distributing a work to justify their running the risks involved in almost any publishing venture—has conflicted with the reading public's "need to know" and its desire for the freest possible flow of information, with publishers' prices for books or other publications the main bone of contention. Such tensions have perhaps been inevitable, because although books, journals, or other traditional kinds of publications are physical commodities, each of which is sold at a particular price, the information they contain is a resource whose value to society is not diminished by the widest possible dissemination.

In their introduction to *Copyright: Intellectual Property in the Information Age*, Ploman and Hamilton explain:

> Copyright has become one of the most complex, technically difficult branches of law, an arcane area populated by experts hiding behind an almost impenetrable jargon. The legal complexities and the language of the experts make it difficult for the general public, for policy- and decision-makers, for technologists and even for practitioners in communication to understand the wider implications of legislation and practice in this field. The resulting failure to formulate coherent policies is serious in a situation where new technologies and changing social patterns alter the conditions for the ordering of cultural life.[2]

Though it must be acknowledged that this branch of law has had to be designed to cover a wide variety of intellectual works and transfers of ownership, it is also clear that many influential book publishers and other major owners of intellectual property have long sought to protect their perceived economic interests by keeping national copyright laws and the relevant international treaties obscure and by dominating discussion of these by governments and international organizations.

The Roots of Copyright

This chapter will focus primarily, though not exclusively, on books. In order to lay the groundwork for its discussion of international copyright concepts and conventions, as well as current issues, it may be useful to provide a brief history of copyright. In ancient cultures, works of the mind did not belong to the individuals or groups who created them but instead to the community and the larger society, with writers and other artists commonly perceived as expressing the collective consciousness of the community rather than their own unique perceptions. This view gradually changed over time in Western societies.

During the Middle Ages, when monasteries bore the primary responsibility for both producing and reproducing Western intellectual works in manuscript form, few of these works carried the name of an author. Gradually, the production, sale, and resale of manuscripts in European countries became better organized and more specialized, spreading literacy and eventually opening the way for users of the newly invented printing press to leapfrog the existing scriptoriums and establish the modern book trade in the fifteenth century.[3]

Although movable type was actually invented in China centuries before Gutenberg was born, his use of movable type on a hand-operated press, in what is now Germany, beginning about 1436 provided the first clear demonstration that books could be reproduced much less expensively and more quickly and easily than they had been by the scribes. With this new technology available to them, printers—the publishers of their day—throughout Europe soon found that publishing books could bring them substantial financial returns. At the same time, however, the arrival of the printing press on the scene increased publishers' risks and up-front costs. Presses were costly, and the large number of copies of each book printed on them sold—or, in some cases, failed to sell—for relatively low prices over a longer period. Competition among book printers intensified, and by the end of the fifteenth century, piracy—the production and sale of editions of books that have not been authorized by their authors in competition with authorized editions—began to emerge as a commercial threat. More and more, publishers thought in terms of guarding the markets for their books.

Not long after the printing press was introduced in Europe, both secular and religious leaders, who clearly perceived the significant influence of widely distributed publications on public opinion, started to regulate the printing trade. They granted favored printers exclusive privileges to publish particular works and by this means were sometimes able to both prevent the publication of works they viewed as undesirable and to censor publications. In England, for example, the Stationers' Company received a royal charter in 1557, which granted it a monopoly on domestic printing and publishing that it maintained for the next 150 years.

At this time, in England and elsewhere in Europe, authors had the right—established by custom rather than law—to be paid for their works, though if they wanted to see them published, they had no choice but to sell them to a government-authorized printer. An author's right to have his work published without distortions or unauthorized alterations was informally recognized, partly because contemporary publishers believed that the economic return on a work would be maximized if it was published as its author intended. Thus, after an author had sold the right to copy one of his works, he retained a measure of control over it.

The Statute of Anne

In the late seventeenth century, England's absolute monarchy was superseded by Parliament, government censorship of publications eased somewhat, and the philosophy of individualism was emerging. Legal protection of an author's copyright began to be more commonly viewed as being validated by natural law. During this same period, the Stationers' Company's tight control over the book trade in England weakened, and the Statute of Anne—the world's first copyright law in the modern sense—was enacted in 1710.[4]

Under the Statute of Anne, authors or any other persons, and not just printers as formerly, could own a copyright. The term of copyright was limited—to twenty-one years for copyrights already in force when the Statute took effect and to fourteen years for all new books, with provision that any of the latter copyrights could be extended for a second fourteen-year term if the relevant book's author were still living when the initial term expired. In order to obtain the copyright protection provided under the Statute—as had been the case under the earlier Stationers' copyright—applicants were required to comply with some formalities: authors had to register books in their own names and to supply free copies of each protected work (sometimes referred to as deposit copies) to several English universities and libraries.

In considering the Statute of Anne or later copyright laws, it is important to bear in mind that, as Ithiel de Sola Pool has so succinctly put it,

> The new notion of intellectual property represented by copyright was rooted in the technology of print. The printing press was a bottleneck where copies could be examined and controlled. In the passage from the author's pen to the reader's hand, the press was the logical place to apply controls, be it to censor sacrilege or sedition or to protect the author's intellectual property.[5]

For modes of reproduction where such an easy locus of control as the printing press did not exist, the concept of copyright was not applied.

Although copyright laws have come to cover many forms of intellectual property besides books over the past several centuries, the need to have a locus of control over the reproduction of works remains the paramount concern in copyright enforcement today.

The Two Principal Approaches to Copyright Law

During the remainder of the eighteenth century and the early nineteenth, copyright laws spread to the rest of Europe and the United States. They generally followed either the Roman-law tradition of France and the rest of continental Europe or the Anglo-Saxon (sometimes referred to as the Anglo-American) legal tradition; these copyright laws, and the traditions they embodied, were subsequently also to strongly influence the copyright laws of metropolitan powers' colonies. Laws following both traditions gave authors the right to sell economic rights in their manuscripts to publishers. Where the traditions differed most markedly was in their approach to protecting the author's moral rights (in French, *droits d'auteur*) in each of his or her works—that is, rights to do such things as control a work's publication or presentation to the public, to control the integrity of a work (i.e., to prevent unauthorized alterations), either to claim authorship of a work or to have it appear anonymously or under a pseudonym, and to withdraw a published work from circulation.

In countries with a Roman-law tradition, the moral rights of authors are—as John Locke and other individualist philosophers advocated—considered to have a basis in natural law and are commonly considered to be both perpetual and inalienable; they are also explicitly protected under copyright law. Countries with an Anglo-Saxon legal tradition also provide protection for the moral rights of authors, but this is generally less extensive than in Roman-law countries and is provided outside of copyright law—for example, through contract law, laws against unfair competition and defamation, and laws protecting citizens' right to privacy. From the Statute of Anne onward, Anglo-Saxon copyright laws have been essentially commercial in character.

The Rise of International Book Piracy

Before the nineteenth century, copyright was principally a domestic concern of European countries, with most books circulating only within the country where they were written and published. After 1800, however, profound social and political changes—such as the rise of the bourgeoisie, the spread of literacy and education, and greater freedom of expression—greatly increased the demand for both literary and artistic works. Publishing expanded rapidly, as did both bookselling and the establishment of libraries. As trade, travel, and communications between countries increased, more and more books and other publications were sold abroad. As these exports grew, however, so did the problem of international piracy. While piracy was a problem in much of Europe, perhaps the pirating of the works of French authors by Belgian and Dutch publishers created the most controversy.[6]

Piracy was rampant not only because of the quick profits it promised but also because intellectual property was still a relatively new concept. Although some earlier Western societies had provided moral and some legal support for the idea of individual authors' or artists' ownership of the intellectual works they created, plagiarism had been commonplace though not esteemed, and copying of works without the author's permission had been widely seen as unethical but not criminal. During the seventeenth and eighteenth centuries, the concept of intellectual property and the idea that it was something deserving legal protection had gradually gained adherents, primarily in Europe. Attitudes toward works of the mind in some other countries, however, were rather different.

For example, in the United States, which adopted its first national copyright law in 1790, reprinting European (primarily English) works without either requesting permission or making payment was widespread in the 1800s. This activity was clearly piracy in the eyes of Europeans, but it was completely legal under U.S. copyright laws of that time, which protected only the works of U.S. authors. The U.S. government had chosen to enable its citizens to obtain copyrighted works from abroad (and the information they contained) at low cost and to encourage the growth of the domestic printing and publishing industries by enabling them to produce books that were proven sellers in England without making payment to copyright holders. The negative side of this policy for the United States was its tendency to discourage the publication of works by U.S. authors, since domestic publishers found the choice between best-selling books by European authors available at no cost and books by lesser-known U.S. authors that would have required payment of royalties an easy one to make.

Emergence of International Copyright Conventions

When printing-press pirates operated from a publisher's own country, the publisher could use its domestic copyright law to shut down their businesses and subject them to penalties; but when the pirates operated from another country, a publisher had no recourse unless the two countries happened to have a bilateral copyright agreement. European countries first made considerable efforts to negotiate such bilateral agreements on the basis of reciprocity of copyright protection, but the resulting web of such agreements proved to be unsatisfactory. Beginning in the 1850s, the idea of a common international framework for copyright protection emerged as the most promising solution. After much preliminary discussion, the International Literary and Artistic Association, a nongovernmental organization (NGO), prepared a draft copyright convention and, at a series of intergovernmental negotiating sessions held in Berne, Switzerland during 1884–86, the International Convention for the Protection of Literary and Artistic Works (1886)—more commonly known as the Berne Convention—was hammered out.

The Berne Convention, whose essential purpose, according to its preamble, is "to protect, in as effective and uniform a manner as possible, the rights of authors in their literary and artistic works," was designed to operate on the principle of *national treatment*: essentially, each member nation of the Berne Union (i.e., a nation adhering to the Convention) will afford copyrighted works originating in *any other* member nation the *same* protection that works originating domestically receive under its own copyright law. The Convention provides that countries adhering to (that is, entering into a legally binding agreement to comply with) it must also provide a minimum standard of protection—in terms of the content, scope, and duration of copyright—to works originating in all Berne Union member nations.

The Berne Union, which began its existence with just 14 members, most of which were European, has expanded over the years to 125 members today. The Convention has undergone quite a few revisions, the most important of which took place in Berlin in 1908, Rome in 1928, Brussels in 1948, Stockholm in 1967, and Paris in 1971. Among other changes, the Berlin revision adopted the principle that no formalities would be required in member countries to obtain copyright protection; the Rome revision added the moral rights of authors to the copyright protection already provided for under the Convention; and the Brussels revision increased the minimum permissible period of copyright protection of a work to the life of its author plus fifty years.[7]

Among the countries of North and South America, only two countries adhered to the Berne Convention in its first few decades: Brazil in 1922 and Canada in 1928. During this period, however, a series of inter-American copyright conventions were developed. These conventions established the principle of national treatment among their members, but because they were open only to countries of the Americas and did not all have the same members, the result was unsatisfactory protection of the works of their members' authors.

World War II, which brought about many changes in the world publishing scene, marked the beginning of a new era in international copyright relations. The United States, which had remained aloof from the Berne Convention primarily because it wished to avoid the suppression of domestic interests that adherence was expected to entail, emerged as a major publishing power and began to take a greater interest in exporting books. (Though the United States did not join Berne until 1989, from 1928 onward U.S. publishers were able to obtain protection of their works under the Convention—without accepting the obligations entailed in adhering to it—by publishing first editions of books simultaneously in the United States and in Canada, the United Kingdom, or another Berne member.) It became interested in the development of a second international convention that would be acceptable to it, the nations of Latin America, and other nations that—mainly because they had so few works produced by their domestic authors and therefore wished to make works produced elsewhere as widely and cheaply available to their citizens as possible—did not wish to accept all of the obligations of Berne adherence. In 1952, the United Nations Educational, Scientific, and Cultural Organization (UNESCO) convened a conference in Geneva to work out such an agreement. The result was the Universal Copyright Convention (UCC), which came into effect in 1955.

The Universal Copyright Convention states that it has three principal purposes: to protect the rights of authors (the sole stated purpose of the Berne Convention); ensure respect for the rights of the individual; and encourage the development of literature, arts, and sciences, as well as the dissemination of works of the mind. Like the Berne Convention, the UCC is based on the principle of national treatment. Unlike Berne, however, it does not provide for a minimum standard of protection of copyrighted works—a characteristic that favors nations that are net importers of intellectual property over those that are net exporters— although the minimum term of copyright protection for books is generally the life of the author plus twenty-five years. The UCC also requires applicants for copyright protection to comply with one formality—namely, putting a notice on the work consisting of three elements— the copyright symbol (©), the name of the copyright owner, and the year of first publication. The UCC, which was signed by forty nations in 1952, currently has ninety-seven members. It has been revised only once, in conjunction with the revision of the Berne Convention, in Paris in 1971.[8]

Developing Countries Confront the International Copyright System

As the colonial empires of Europe broke up with the granting of independence to former colonies in the 1940s, 50s, and 60s, large numbers of new, often weak nations appeared and set about the business of fostering their own economic development. Although these nations' resource endowments, climates, infrastructures, education levels, and political philosophies varied widely, they generally agreed that they would need to obtain scientific, technical, and other information—much of which was in the form of copyrighted works—from the industrial nations if they were to realize their hopes for development. A publication of UNESCO notes:

> Improvement of living conditions everywhere depends to a large extent on the progress of education, science and culture. Such progress is made possible through the dissemination of information and knowledge and its application to national

development. Intellectual production is just as important to the process of nation-building as material production, providing as it does the foundation for all advancement.⁹

More generally, Third World countries sought to decrease their dependence on the information production and distribution system largely controlled by the industrial powers, since this offered hope of removing, or at least lessening, the fundamental inequalities between the two groups of nations.

As developing nations attempted to acquire more information from the industrial nations, the former's very limited means posed a major obstacle, as did the reluctance of many publishers and other producers of information products in industrial countries to give up existing or potential overseas markets. UNESCO's *The ABC of Copyright* explains:

> In the 1960s, developing countries under great pressure to meet the educational needs of their people found that they were having difficulty obtaining rights to translate and reproduce needed educational materials. The needs of these countries were brought to the attention of the publishing countries where the rights were held. Developing countries ... said that copyright was blocking access to translation and reproduction of such works. The copyright owners, authors, and publishers in the major publishing nations countered that authors [and publishers] were entitled to a fair return for their work and that their rights should be respected.¹⁰

Prices of books produced in industrial countries naturally reflected their own costs—wage levels, materials costs, etc.—and the consumers' ability to pay in their own domestic and primary export markets. Because copyrighted books published in industrial countries were very expensive in the context of developing countries—both because of their high cost of manufacture and, in some instances, because of price gouging by local distributors—book pirates found ready markets for their unauthorized editions of, for example, bestselling U.S. or European textbooks. New technological developments—for example, in offset printing and binding equipment and in reprography—and improved air and surface transport services permitted pirates to operate on a larger scale and to increase their returns. Copyright laws in developing countries were sometimes nonexistent, more often loosely drawn when it came to protection of foreign works, and tended to be loosely enforced.[11]

Industrial countries, the United States the most prominent among them, attempted to meet the needs of Third World countries for low-priced books through a variety of foreign aid programs that subsidized the export of their publishers' books or subsidized the production of reprints or translations abroad. Privately financed aid programs also contributed to this effort. These programs reached their peak in the 1960s and delivered millions of books. They received mixed reviews, however: they certainly helped to meet developing countries' growing needs for information, but they were also criticized for inhibiting the growth of indigenous publishing in the recipient countries—another means by which these countries hoped to reduce their dependence on industrial country publishers. Western publishers also attempted—and still, to a certain extent, do so today—to cope with piracy of their books and to meet developing countries' book needs by selling them "international student editions" or "Asian editions" at prices well below those charged for the same works in their home markets.[12]

Meanwhile, in various international forums—including UNESCO, the administrator of the UCC; the United International Bureaux for the Protection of Intellectual Property (known as BIRPI, the acronym based on the French version of the organization's name), then the administrator of the Berne Convention; and the United Nations Conference on Trade and Development (UNCTAD)—developing countries, using their combined voting strength and enlisting the support of some sympathetic publishers and government officials in industrial countries, pressed for a lessening of their economic inequality with the industrial countries (the "new international economic order") and, more particularly, a reduction in industrial countries' control of information production and distribution (the "new world information order").

The Stockholm and Paris Conferences

In 1963, an African copyright meeting held in Brazzaville (in what today is the Republic of Congo) first suggested that the Berne Convention be modified to give developing countries easier access to copyrighted works originating in industrial countries. This suggestion was pushed hard by developing countries before and during the 1967 Stockholm Conference held to discuss revision of Berne. After difficult and protracted negotiations, agreement was reached on a Protocol Regarding Developing Countries, which was annexed to the Berne Convention. At the same conference, the World Intellectual Property Organization (WIPO) was created to succeed BIRPI as the administrator of the Berne Convention. In 1974, WIPO became a specialized agency of the United Nations.

The Stockholm Protocol allowed several exceptions to the generally high level of protection provided to the copyrighted works of Berne Union members in order to assist developing countries. Among other things, it reduced the maximum term of protection of copyrighted works sought by developing countries from the life of the author plus fifty years to the life of the author plus twenty-five years; reduced restrictions on access to material developing countries needed for education and research; provided for compulsory licenses—licenses provided by developing country governments to their domestic publishers in consultation with, but not necessarily with the consent of, the publishers or authors holding the rights—to translate or reproduce copyrighted works in return for what was considered equitable payment in the developing country concerned.

The Stockholm Protocol, conceived in controversy, failed to satisfy either developing or industrial countries. Ploman and Hamilton observe:

> In the eyes of the developing countries, the Protocol bore the stamp of the industrialized world since everything had been done [during its negotiation] to incorporate the changes suggested by the industrialized countries so as to make the Protocol acceptable to them. . . . In the developed countries, there were even stronger reactions against the Protocol. The Protocol was said to permit legalized piracy, to single out one section of the public—i.e., authors and publishers—for sacrifices on behalf of the developing countries and so to dilute the level of protection that the result would be a dissolution of the Berne Union.[13]

Most industrial countries refused to ratify the Protocol. Many substantial industrial country publishers, reacting to a perceived threat to their overseas markets, stepped up their efforts to protect the copyrights they held. National publishers' associations in industrial countries became more deeply involved in international copyright issues, as did the International Publishers Association, headquartered in Geneva. In addition, the International Group of Scientific, Technical & Medical

Publishers (STM), headquartered in Amsterdam, was founded in 1968 partly to enable its members to better protect their copyrights.

Since the developing and industrial countries were stalemated in their dispute over the Stockholm Protocol, it was decided in 1969 that the best way forward would be to convene a joint conference for simultaneous revision of both the Berne Convention and the UCC. This conference, which was held in Paris in 1971, worked out a compromise between industrial and developing countries on the latter's use of copyrighted works for nonprofit educational and research purposes. The Paris revisions, which were formally ratified in 1974, apply to publishers in developing countries that are members of Berne or the UCC and that have brought their domestic copyright laws into conformity with the compulsory licensing provisions of either or both copyright conventions. Under them, such publishers may reprint or translate works—subject to more extensive restrictions than had been included in the Stockholm Protocol—owned by copyright holders in industrial country members of Berne or the UCC. Developing countries thus obtained a significant, though limited, concession in Paris from industrial countries, which agreed to compulsory licensing partly out of fear that developing countries might opt out of the international copyright system, creating serious disorder in the international book trade, if none of their principal demands were met. Industrial countries, on the other hand, generally viewed the various restrictions placed on compulsory licenses under the Paris revisions as essential means of protecting the rights of their authors and publishers.

Compulsory Licensing

Under the Paris revisions, compulsory licenses, which can be issued only by a developing country's national copyright authority, are available to a publisher in a developing country provided the originating publisher or other copyright holder:
1. has been allowed a period (generally one to three years for translations, three to seven years for reproductions) of exclusive publication rights;
2. has not made an edition of the book available in the developing country at a cost considered reasonable in that market; and
3. has been contacted by the developing country publisher about the possible purchase of a normal (voluntary) license to re-

print or translate but has either failed to respond during a prescribed waiting period or declined to sell such a license.

Compulsory licenses are nonexclusive and nontransferable, and require the licensee to make royalty payments to the copyright holder—in internationally convertible currency—that are in keeping with those paid under voluntary licenses negotiated between publishers in the two countries. Translated works published under a compulsory license must be used only for purposes of teaching, scholarship, or research, while reproduced works published under such a license may be used only in connection with systematic instructional activities; these terms are, however, open to a variety of interpretations. Such works may not be sold for profit, must be produced in the publisher's own country (except in cases where the country lacks the necessary publishing infrastructure), and usually may not be exported.

Despite the big head of steam behind compulsory licensing at both the Stockholm and Paris conferences, relatively few developing countries have granted compulsory licenses to their publishers since 1971. Nonetheless, the ability of any developing country belonging to Berne or the UCC to enact compulsory licensing legislation increases the leverage of *all* developing country publishers in negotiating normal (voluntary) licenses with publishers from industrial countries. At the same time, it must be pointed out that developing countries' wide-ranging campaign for additional concessions to help create a new international economic order and a new world information order subsequently encountered stiff resistance from conservative industrial country governments, especially during the 1980s, and was effectively, though not permanently, halted. Although most industrial country publishers have come to accept compulsory licensing as a fact of life in the international book trade, they generally have sought to head off the issuance of compulsory licenses in developing countries by either issuing a low-cost edition of their own in that market or, more commonly, negotiating a voluntary licensing agreement with a local publisher.

There are several reasons for such actions by industrial country publishers. First, despite their countries' adherence to Berne and/or the UCC, some publishers object to compulsory licensing on the grounds that it interferes with the operation of markets. Second, publishers have had a number of problems with developing countries' implementation of compulsory licensing. In a 1992 issue of *Publishing Research Quarterly*, Lynette Owen, rights and contracts director for the Longman Group U.K. Ltd (now part of Addison Wesley Longman), comments:

> Although countries such as India have introduced compulsory licensing which is broadly in line with the provisions of Paris, some other countries that are members of one or both of the conventions have introduced legislation that in no way complies with those requirements.... With local legislation of this kind, anyone dealing with reprint applications from such countries must be aware that a blunt refusal of a [voluntary] license may result in a reprint edition appearing anyway, with inevitable effects on sales of the original edition to the market.[14]

Third, publishers have had a number of significant technical problems with developing countries' implementation of compulsory licenses, including delayed payment of royalties, taxation of royalties, and illegal exportation of books produced under compulsory licenses. Determining which portion of such difficulties is owing to the inefficiency and limited infrastructure—as viewed by someone from an industrial country—of a developing country and its publishing sector, and which portion is owing to the deliberate actions of a local publisher and/or the country's government, can be quite problematic for faraway industrial country publishers.

Publishers Launch an Offensive against Book Piracy

Book piracy continued to expand during the 1960s, 70s, and early 80s as technological improvements in manufacturing and shipping, and strong economic growth in parts of the developing world, especially Asia, created many opportunities. While figures on the volume of piracy—like figures on the drug trade, capital flight, or other illegal activities—are extremely difficult to obtain, it is clear that total annual losses of all copyright proprietors in industrial countries—including, among others, producers of films, videocassettes, audiotapes, compact disks, computer hardware and software, and books—from piracy of their works were quite substantial, amounting to a billion dollars a year or more in the early 1980s. Book piracy accounted for a substantial fraction of this: for example, 1984 figures released by the International Intellectual Property Alliance (IIPA)—a group of North American industry associations whose members produce copyrighted works—indicate that total losses by U.S. and Canadian publishers from piracy in the top ten countries serving as bases for this activity amounted to $427 million.

Publishers in industrial countries, which had long been concerned about piracy and its effects on their balance sheets, became sufficiently alarmed during the early 1980s to push for, and obtain, strong action by their conservative, probusiness governments to combat piracy. The United Kingdom negotiated with several Asian nations known to harbor major producers of pirated books, videocassettes, films, computer software, etc. in order to win amendments in, and improved enforcement of, their copyright laws. At the urging of the IIPA (which includes the Association of American Publishers among its members) and other knowledge industry representatives, the U.S. government used the leverage created by the trade preferences and foreign aid it grants developing countries to convince such major pirate bases as Taiwan, Korea, Singapore, Malaysia, Indonesia, and the Dominican Republic to bring their copyright laws into conformity with the two major conventions and to beef up both enforcement of, and sanctions for violators under, these laws.

New legal provisions, particularly those enacted as a result of diplomatic and commercial pressure from overseas, have not always been energetically or effectively enforced, but, on balance, considerable progress has been made against book piracy in developing countries. Such piracy is now widely seen as declining, though far from eradicated. For example, the IIPA's 1988 figure for losses of U.S. and Canadian publishers owing to piracy in the top ten countries serving as pirate bases was $222 million, down $205 million compared with losses four years earlier. At the same time, however, industrial countries clearly are becoming increasingly concerned about piracy in the countries of Eastern and Central Europe, as well as the states of the former Soviet Union, as their socialist economies and legal systems come to resemble those of Western Europe.

Many publishers in industrial countries recognize, however, that piracy can only be minimized or eliminated over the long haul by reducing the economic incentives that brought the pirates into publishing in the first place. In recent years, publishers in the industrial world have responded to piracy (including illegal photocopying as well as traditional printing-press piracy) and compulsory licensing by making greater efforts to sell their own books in developing countries at affordable prices and to sell reprint and translation rights—that is, to sell negotiated (voluntary) licenses—more reasonably than they had in the past. Nonetheless, conflicts between the interests of the industrial country publishers and developing countries clearly remain. For example, Lynette Owen advised fellow industrial country publishers:

> In some countries student texts are adopted [ordered for classroom use] in large quantities in the original English edition; in such cases the appearance of a local translation could have a very significant effect on sales. . . . and in some cases it may be prudent to withhold rights. More units may be sold of a translated edition, but the resulting royalty income may well be less than the income derived from the fewer sales of the English edition.[15]

Although the business logic of such a statement is unassailable, the negative impact such an approach to selling rights is likely to have on both education in developing countries and the long-run growth of their book markets is not difficult to discern.

As printing-press piracy has diminished in recent years, the knotty problem of unauthorized photocopying of copyrighted works in developing countries has received greater attention. In developing countries, as in industrial countries, the reproduction of copyrighted material without permission or payment is commonplace. Indeed, after many years of having had the freedom to make copies for personal or commercial use, many individuals and firms have come to consider such copying a personal right. There are also copy shops that reproduce numerous copies of whole books, chapters, or periodical articles for resale. These operations may operate around the clock and sometimes even rival printing-press pirates in the quantity of their output. Publishers whose books have been copied have sustained significant losses, though it should be pointed out that the combined losses to publishers from printing-press piracy and illegal photocopying are dwarfed by copyright holders' losses from the piracy of such products as audiotapes, videocassettes, compact disks, and computer software.

Industrial country publishers, with finite resources at their disposal, have had to concentrate most of their antipiracy efforts abroad on combating printing-press piracy rather than the much more frequent but smaller-scale photocopying infringements. Nonetheless, as an extension of their efforts to control unauthorized photocopying in their home markets through national collecting agencies, also known as reproduction rights organizations (RROs)—e.g., the Copyright Clearance Center in the United States, the Copyright Licensing Agency in the United Kingdom, VG Wort in Germany, Kopinpor in Norway, and CEDRO in

Spain—set up to collect royalties for the reproduction of copyrighted works, industrial countries have created the International Federation of Reproduction Rights Organizations (IFRRO). In addition to its primary purpose of promoting protection of the copyrights administered by each of its member RROs—providing a mechanism for royalties for copying done outside a publisher's home country to be collected locally and then remitted by the local RRO to the publisher's domestic RRO—IFRRO has sought to encourage developing countries to set up their own RROs.

As RROs have attempted to grapple with the photocopying problem nationally and internationally, many though not all industrial country publishers have concluded that charging users (especially large, institutional ones) on a transactional basis—that is, charging them individually for each copy made—is not feasible and that, consequently, collectively licensing large users—that is, charging them a fixed license fee for all of their copying (strictly speaking, only the copying of those works for which rights are administered by the RRO) during a specific period—is the only practical way to collect royalties.

Electronic Publishing Roils the Waters

When the Internet was originally used principally for electronic mail exchanges and file transfers among scholars and, later, also for publication of textual information (without graphics) on gopher sites, there were only a limited number of users and almost all of the information exchanged was noncommercial in character. The attitudes of Internet users generally reflected the cooperative ethic of scholarly communication, with information sharing commonplace and unrestricted access to information widely encouraged. In recent years, however, the increasing popularity of the Internet, both for e-mail exchanges and for obtaining access to information published on the World Wide Web that is readable using graphical browser software (Netscape Navigator, Microsoft Internet Explorer, Mosaic, and others) has brought commercial concerns—and, with them, copyright issues—to the fore.

The ease with which the new technologies allow copies to be made of information published electronically (digitally)—on the Web, through electronic bulletin boards, from proprietary databases, and so on—and then downloaded to a user's personal computer and transmitted by them to other users' PCs has been a boon to both scholarly and commercial communication and a cause of serious concern to publishers and other owners of intellectual property. On the one hand, owners of copyrighted information are attracted by the large audiences they can reach by publishing and distributing their works electronically; on the other hand, they are alarmed by the risks of information being obtained by many users without permission or payment. For their part, many information users—and especially those in developing and transition countries and their governments—wish to obtain the maximum benefit from the new publishing and communications technologies but fear being prevented from doing so not only by the costs of the equipment and training required but also by the charges levied by copyright owners for the use of information. At the same time, the scholarly community, the manufacturers of electronics and communications equipment, and various providers of telecommunication services, such as telephone companies and Internet service providers (ISPs), strongly support the broadest possible access of users to information by electronic means. Although there is doubtless some risk in making statements about the views of general publics in various countries on these issues, it is clear that publics also favor broad access to electronic information. The diverse views of the affected parties have thus set the stage for a replaying—hopefully, in a less strident form—of the debate on the uses of copyrighted printed works (described earlier) that created considerable controversy during the 1960s and 70s.

Over the last several years, individual publishers and their national and international associations have put considerable effort into developing technical means to ensure their control over copyrighted information in electronic form. They have sought to develop electronic rights management systems (ERMS) to monitor and license interactive uses of copyrighted material—that is, uses made of such material in which users choose when and where they will receive it. Publishers' efforts to "brand" their copyrighted material have resulted in the creation of various systems, some of which are currently being tested. For example, digital codes embedded in the material would enable the publisher to track users and to require payment, if desired, before the material could be used (for example, requiring receipt of payment before making encrypted material readable). The basic concept these systems seek to establish in the electronic environment, then, is transactional licensing—that is, customers pay for each use made of the copyrighted material.[16]

In an electronic environment where many fear that blanket licensing arrangements will offer insufficient protection against unauthorized and uncompensated uses of intellectual property, publishers are embracing ERMs eagerly. For instance, at the annual Frankfurt Book Fair in October 1997, demonstrations of the digital object identifier (DOI) system, an ERMS that has been developed under the sponsorship of the Association of American Publishers and more recently has been supported by the International Publishers Association, won glowing praise from publishers, especially those specializing in STM subjects. Dietrich Götze, chief executive of Axel Springer Verlag, described the development of such systems as "one of the most important events in publishing for this century," and Gerhard Kurtze, president of the Börsenverein (the German publishers association), termed it "surely the most significant structural shift in academic and scientific publishing since Gutenberg."[17]

Electronic management systems pose some serious problems, however, and their widespread implementation is far from certain. For one thing, they raise serious privacy questions: will users of copyrighted works find it acceptable for copyright owners or some national or international administering body acting on their behalf to know what material they are using, as well as when and where they are using it? For another, the system of "pay per view" for copyrighted works in digital form that ERMSs could make possible would not allow users any of the "fair use" rights—to make certain limited uses of copyrighted works for various noncommercial purposes (including teaching, scholarship, and preservation by libraries) without having to pay royalties— currently specified in countries' copyright laws and also established through relevant case law. A third difficulty ERMs are quite likely to face if they are extensively used is the devising of electronic means of getting around them—of allowing users to gain unauthorized access to information in which the publishers' digital codes are embedded. Interestingly, these potential difficulties with ERMs are quite similar to those that arose a couple of decades ago when publishers attempted, with little success, to find a way to control the photocopying of their printed works by various technological means.

Negotiation of a New WIPO Treaty

In December 1996, after several years of discussion, negotiations on a new WIPO treaty intended to adapt international copyright practices to the new world of digital technologies and communication, were completed in Geneva. Controversy arose, especially in the final stages of negotiations, as a result of the fundamental disagreements some major industrial country governments and copyright owners had with an ad hoc alliance of developing country governments and the various groups in industrial countries (mentioned above) who opposed copyright owners' plans to extend their control over uses made of works they publish in digital form.

In a somewhat unexpected turn of events, the copyright owners and their governmental supporters were soundly defeated in most of their efforts to get agreements passed to enhance their control over works they publish in digital form. Attempts to make an incidental copy of a digital work produced in the random access memory (RAM) of a user's computer—by, for example, downloading a page from a copyrighted Web page—subject to the control of the copyright owner failed, as did efforts to eliminate for digital works the "fair use" exceptions to copyright owners' rights that are currently provided for under various national copyright laws. Copyright owners' and their supporters' efforts to make intermediaries in the transmission of digital works (for example, Internet service providers) liable for copyright infringements by their customers—to force them to serve, in effect, as copyright police—also failed.[18]

Various improvements in the protection of copyrighted works were, in fact, enacted in the treaty: for example, the applicability of Article 9 of the Berne Convention, which covers reproduction rights in copyrighted works and permissible exceptions to these, to digital works was clearly spelled out; the scope of protection for computer programs and original databases, and intellectual property owners' right of rental were clarified; it was made clear that infringement of any right covered by the treaty or the Berne Convention applies to both copyright owners' exclusive rights and their rights to be remunerated for uses made of their works; and the duration of copyright protection of photographic works was extended from twenty-five to fifty years.[19] Nonetheless, what didn't go into the new WIPO treaty was considerably more important than what went into it. The treaty has now gone out to WIPO's member countries for ratification and any amendments of their domestic copyright laws that may be necessary to bring them into compliance with the treaty's provisions.

At the December 1996 diplomatic conference at which the WIPO Copyright Treaty was agreed upon, a draft treaty was presented on intellectual property in nonoriginal databases, which was supported by intellectual property interests and their governmental supporters but opposed by numerous other groups, including many from the international educational and scientific communities. Owing to the controversy and the lack of time available to consider the implications of the *sui generis* protection of databases (that is, a right of ownership in databases that would be inherent, regardless of their originality, which is seen by its advocates as justified by the work done and expenditures incurred by their proprietors in assembling and maintaining them), the treaty was put aside for subsequent consideration.

In September 1997, WIPO held a three-day information meeting on intellectual property in databases in Geneva. It was characterized by wide-ranging discussions of the subject, and, in the words of the report adopted by the meeting:

> Many delegations stated that they needed more time for further study and consultations on national, regional and international level [sic], and they stated that they needed further analysis to assess the need for such a system; furthermore these delegations pleaded for caution and [a] slower pace for international deliberations.[20]

The meeting therefore decided that the International Bureau of WIPO should thoroughly consider the discussions held at the information meeting and the issues raised, accept further submissions on relevant topics from member governments and other interested parties, and report back to its member countries on these by September 1998. Because of the preliminary stage of debate, no date was set for a future WIPO meeting on intellectual property in databases.

Developing Countries Shift Their Perspectives

While industrial country governments and their publishers have stepped up their efforts to combat book piracy in recent years, the economic and social development of some developing countries and the advancement of their publishing industries have induced them to change their attitudes toward the international copyright system. When a country reaches the point where it has substantial numbers of copyrights of its own authors and publishers to protect, it often becomes convinced that joining and strictly adhering to international conventions are in its own best interests. Dina Malhotra, founder of Hind Pocket Books (New Delhi), observed in a recent article that India—once a leading copyright outlaw in the eyes of industrial country publishers—"now has to protect the copyrights of its own nationals as well as foreigners' rights. It also has to seek protection internationally for its own copyrights for books and audio- and video-tapes which have also become victims of widespread piracy in many Asian countries."[21] Among other countries, Korea, Taiwan, and the members of the Association of Southeast Asian Nations have recently shifted their stances on international copyright issues for similar reasons.

Efforts to Include Intellectual Property in the GATT

In addition to their increased direct efforts to combat piracy over the past decade, industrial country publishers—which have grown increasingly impatient with what they view as weak enforcement and inadequate protection of their rights under Berne and the UCC—have persuaded their generally conservative governments, some of which perceived copyright concessions granted to developing countries as inappropriate international welfare schemes, to press in new international forums for better protection of copyrighted works. These efforts can be viewed as part of a broader attempt by industrial countries to rein in international organizations and to use these bodies more deliberately to pursue their own, sometimes rather narrowly defined (national) economic and political interests. During the protracted (eight-year) Uruguay Round of multilateral trade negotiations that took place under the General Agreement on Tariffs and Trade (GATT), which has its headquarters in Geneva, industrial countries worked to arrange inclusion of works of intellectual property for the first time. Katerina Czarnecki, vice president and director of International Rights for Macmillan Publishing Company (New York), recently explained that industrial country publishers—despite considerable differences among them on some issues—had three principal goals in these negotiations:
1. an agreement on standards of protection to be based on the levels of protection now in the Berne Convention;
2. an agreement on standards of enforcement which would ensure that adequate and effective enforcement mechanisms are available to copyright owners, including accessible civil remedies and strong deterrent criminal sanctions for piracy; and
3. an agreement on a dispute-settlement mechanism allowing signatory states injured by another state's failure to live up to new standards of protection and enforcement to take the offending state to a GATT dispute-settlement panel.[22]

While developing countries and their publishers increased their involvement in the international copyright system over the past couple of decades, they generally resisted the proposed spreading of international copyright jurisdiction to encompass not only WIPO and UNESCO but also the GATT, primarily because they feared that the GATT dispute-settlement mechanism would be used against them, with the consequence that their access to the copyrighted works of industrial countries would be further restricted.

In April 1994, the Uruguay Round negotiations were formally concluded in Marrakech, Morocco, with the signing of the Final Act by representatives of more than 120 countries. After receiving approval from enough participating countries' legislatures, the Final Act came into effect in January 1995.

When the Final Act came into effect, publishers (and other owners of intellectual property) from industrial countries won inclusion of provisions designed to accomplish their three principal goals. In copyright matters, the agreement requires all participants to comply with the substantive provisions of the Paris revision of the Berne Convention, though they will not be required to protect moral rights as specified in Berne's Article 6. Participants must provide procedures under their domestic laws to ensure that intellectual property rights can be effectively enforced by both their own citizens and foreign rights holders. The agreement also set up a Council for Trade-Related Aspects of Intellectual Property Rights, more commonly known as the TRIPS Council, to monitor the agreement's operations and governments' compliance with it. Any disputes concerning intellectual property rights are dealt with under the dispute-settlement procedure of the World Trade Organization (WTO), the organization that succeeded the GATT when the Final Act came into effect. The Final Act also contains a most-favored-nation clause that requires any participating country that grants a concession, in an agreement on intellectual property rights, to nationals of another country to immediately grant the same concession to nationals of all other participating countries; exceptions to this practice are permitted, however, in certain circumstances.

Once the Final Act came into effect, developed (industrial) countries had one year—that is, until January 1996—to bring their domestic legislation and practices into conformity with the agreement's provisions. Developing countries are allowed longer transition periods: developing countries and countries switching from centrally planned to market-based economies will have five years (until January 2000), and the least developed (poorest) countries—as designated by the

United Nations—will have eleven years (until January 2006), to achieve conformity.

At this writing, it is clear that copyright holders from the major industrial countries have, through negotiation, wrested important concessions from users of intellectual property in developing countries. It will not be possible to know how international flows of copyrighted materials will actually be affected, however, until more experience is gained with application of the Final Act's provisions and the use of the WTO's dispute-settlement mechanism. Thus far, only four cases concerning copyrighted intellectual property have been brought to the WTO's Dispute Settlement Body—the United States has brought all of these cases, which concern separate disputes with Canada, Denmark, Ireland, and Sweden—and none of these have been settled yet. Another influence on the settlement of intellectual property disputes may be the mediation service that WIPO, whose experience with intellectual property matters is considerably greater than that of the WTO, is offering to perform, for a fee, in such disputes.

Longtime Holdouts Have Joined the Berne Convention

Although the 1971 Paris revisions brought the Berne Convention and the UCC closer together, substantial differences between them have remained. Though there has long been some support—especially in Europe, the cradle of the Berne Convention—for the idea of merging the two conventions, this has not happened, primarily because of continuing differences in the needs of industrial and developing countries. Nonetheless, U.S. unhappiness with, and withdrawal from, UNESCO in the early 1980s—though the United States remains a member of the UCC—plus its increasing consciousness of U.S. interests in defending the intellectual property rights of its firms and authors—fostered by vigorous lobbying by associations of copyright proprietors in the book, film, audio, television, computer, and other "knowledge industries"—finally induced it to become a Berne member in 1989.

After the United States joined Berne, several countries in both Latin America and the Caribbean, and Africa followed suit. China, which had never been part of the world copyright system, and did not have even a domestic copyright law until rather recently,[23] joined both the UCC and Berne in 1992. The Russian Federation, which maintains UCC membership as one of the successor states to the former Soviet Union (which joined that convention only in 1973), joined Berne in March

1995. The Republic of Korea joined Berne in 1996, and Indonesia in September 1997. With these longtime holdouts now clearly within the international copyright fold, it continues to be true—despite strenuous and ongoing disagreements about how copyright should be applied in the world of digital publishing—that, as Philip Altbach wrote in 1986, "despite the stresses, some piracy, and the lukewarm adherence of some Third World nations, the international copyright system appears to be accepted as the basic structure to regulate the international flow of knowledge."[24]

Notes

This chapter was originally published in *International Book Publishing: An Encyclopedia*, edited by Philip G. Altbach and Edith S. Hoshino (New York: Garland Publishing, 1995), and extensively revised and updated for this book. The views expressed in this chapter are those of its author and should not be interpreted as reflecting the views of his employer, The International Monetary Fund.

[1] Edward W. Ploman and L. Clark Hamilton, *Copyright: Intellectual Property in the Information Age* (London: Routledge & Kegan Paul, 1980), 1.
[2] Ibid., 2.
[3] The discussion of the early history of copyright in the preceding two paragraphs follows that in Ploman and Hamilton, *Copyright: Intellectual Property*, 4–9.
[4] Lyman Ray Patterson, *Copyright in Historical Perspective* (Nashville, Tennessee: Vanderbilt University Press, 1968), 6–7.
[5] Ithiel de Sola Pool, *Technologies of Freedom* (London: Belknap Press of Harvard University Press, 1983), 16–17.
[6] Ploman and Hamilton, *Copyright: Intellectual Property*, 18–19.
[7] For a more extensive description of the Berne Convention's provisions, see Claude Colombet, *Major Principles of Copyright and Neighbouring Rights in the World: A Comparative Law Approach* (Paris: UNESCO, 1987), 105–19.
[8] For a more extensive description of the Universal Copyright Convention's provision, see Colombet, *Major Principles of Copyright*, 119–24.
[9] United Nations Educational, Scientific, and Cultural Organization, *The ABC of Copyright* (Paris: UNESCO, 1981), 67.
[10] Ibid., 68.
[11] For a more detailed description of developing countries' interactions with the international copyright system, see Philip G. Altbach, "Knowledge Enigma: The Context of Copyright in the Third World," chap. 6, in Philip G. Altbach, *The Knowledge Context: Comparative Perspectives on the Distribution of Knowledge* (Albany: State University of New York Press, 1987), 85–112.
[12] For a more detailed description of U.S. government assistance provided for publishing in developing countries, see William M. Childs and Donald E. McNeil, eds., *American Books Abroad: Toward a National Policy* (Washington, D.C.: Helen Dwight Reid Educational Foundation, 1986).
[13] Ploman and Hamilton, *Copyright: Intellectual Property*, 62.
[14] Lynette Owen, "Exploiting the Rights in the Agreement," *Publishing Research Quarterly* 8, no. 2 (summer 1992): 56.
[15] Ibid., 57.

[16] For further information on electronic rights management systems (ERMSs), see Daniel J. Gervais, "Electronic Rights Management Systems (ERMS): The Next Logical Step in the Evolution of Rights Management" (paper presented at a conference held in Seville, Spain in May 1997). It can be found on the World Wide Web, on the (U.S.) Copyright Clearance Center's site, at http://www.copyright.com/stuff/ecms_network.htm. See also Clifford Lynch, "Identifiers and Their Role in Networked Information Applications," in the Association of Research Libraries' *ARL: A Bimonthly Newsletter of Research Library Issues*, no. 194 (October 1997), 12–16.

[17] Doreen Carvajal, "Electronic 'Branding' Receives Accolades at the Frankfurt Book Fair," *New York Times*, October 20, 1997, D11.

[18] For an interesting, though clearly partisan, discussion of the background to, and the actual WIPO Treaty negotiations at, the Geneva conference, see two articles that appeared, under the heading "Confab Clips Copyright Cartel," in the March 1997 issue (Vol. 5, No. 3) of *Wired* magazine: Pamela Samuelson, "Big Media Beaten Back," pp. 61–64; and John Browning, "Africa 1, Hollywood 0," 61–64.

[19] For further details on the copyright treaty that emerged from the December 1996 Geneva conference, see World Intellectual Property Organization, "Diplomatic Conference on Certain Copyright and Neighboring Rights Questions: Agreed Statements Concerning the WIPO Copyright Treaty," WIPO Document No. CRNR/DC/6 (English), December 23, 1996, available on WIPO's Web site at http://www.wipo.org/eng/diplconf/distrib/96dc.htm. See also WIPO Press Release No. 106 (English), (untitled), December 20, 1996, available on WIPO's Web site at http://www.wipo.org/eng/diplconf/distrib/press106.htm.

[20] World Intellectual Property Organization, Information Meeting on Intellectual Property in Databases, Paragraph 10 (chairman's summary of the discussion) of "Report adopted by the Information Meeting," WIPO Document No. DB/IM/6 (English), page 3, available on WIPO's Web site at http://www.wipo.org/eng/meetings/infdat97/db_im_6.htm.

[21] Dina N. Malhotra, "Publishing and Copyright in India," *Rights* 5, no. 4 (1991–92): 1.

[22] Katerina Czarnecki, "Enforcing Copyright Law Within and Between Nations," *Publishing Research Quarterly* 8, no. 2 (summer 1992): 28.

[23] For an interesting discussion of Chinese attitudes toward the Western, individualist concept of intellectual property, see Ploman and Hamilton, *Copyright: Intellectual Property*, pp. 140–47. For further information on how and why attitudes toward, and protection of, intellectual property vary so widely among countries, see Donald B. Marron and David G. Steel, "Which Countries Protect Intellectual Property? An Empirical Analysis of Software Piracy," University of Chicago, Graduate School of Business, October 1997.

[24] Altbach, *Knowledge Enigma*, 112.

5

Distribution: The Neglected Link in the Publishing Chain

Amadio A. Arboleda

Surveys of publishing in the Third World tend to be narrow for two basic reasons: publishing in the Third World is narrowly aimed, and data on it are noticeably lacking. Distribution is consistently neglected in surveys of Third World publishing. Many statistical overviews present a plethora of numbers on manufacturing and production, but there is almost nothing on what happens with the product. This is paradoxical because, as a number of book experts have pointed out, a book does not fulfill its purpose until it is read, and to be read it must reach a reader. This is where distribution becomes all important. Distribution is difficult in the industrialized countries as well as in Third World countries. The major difference is that distribution problems in Third World countries often take on the proportions of a crisis.

The difficulties of distribution stem from the very craft of creating and producing the written materials of communication in the form of books. The craft is a complicated one, far more complex than many of the processes that give us some of the well-known products of modern society. Marshall Lee writes that "the bookmaker has two basic tasks: (a) to facilitate communication between author and reader, and (b) to make the book a successful commercial product. Publishers," he points out, "often have cultural or personal objectives when they accept a book for publication, but the object of publishing as a business is to *sell* books."[1] Although Lee's view of a book as a commercial product is somewhat restrictive because it does not spell out the social and cultural roles of publishing, he tries to show us that the intricate process of facilitating reader-author communication involves both the shaping and creation of a book *and* getting the book into the hands of a reader. He also points out, nevertheless, that "it is only in the profit motive that book publishing resembles any other business. It is much more informal, complicated, and hazardous than most."[2] This business aspect and the hazardous nature of the publishing enterprise in general is recognized in the Third World, but there is very little awareness of its creative role, particularly in relation to culture and education.

Lee then goes on to show the essential difference between publishing and other economic endeavors by making a comparison between books and a very necessary and standard consumer product, toothpaste. The process of creating and selling a consumer product involves "manufacturers [hiring] people to create a few products to their desire [after considerable market research], [standardizing] their manufacture, and [turning] them out in large quantities year after year."[3] The accompanying promotion campaigns, he points out, are set up to encourage buyers to purchase the product. Once the campaigns are effective they can be used over and over again. "The products are sold in stores accessible to virtually everyone and their production can be geared to their sales—or at least to an estimate of sales based on thorough research. Most important, a satisfied customer is likely to continue buying the same product more or less indefinitely."[4]

A Peculiar Product: The Book

In contrast to other enterprises, the products that publishers sell are not standardized. Each book is unique. This means that a publisher, unlike the toothpaste manufacturer, has many products to sell, each one different and each one "a unique creation by an independent individual who has determined personally what the products shall be."[5] In addition, the sale of a book does not insure that the buyer will remain a steady customer of the publisher. This is quite unlike other commercial endeavors wherein a customer, if satisfied, will often continue to patronize a certain product and its producer. It is incumbent, therefore, on the publisher to try to cultivate as many distribution outlets as possible including, in addition to the usual channels of bookstores and wholesalers, government institutions, educational institutions, libraries, and book clubs.

Distribution is further hampered because publishers in Third World countries are often not well versed in the intricacies of consumer demand and, therefore, do not know how many people will buy a book. As a result they tend to produce uneconomically small quantities. Their limited production quantities are, of course, based on other factors: experience with low sales because potential buyers cannot afford to purchase books or do not consider books a primary need; high cost of raw materials, such as paper and printing ink; the limited number of available sales outlets, particularly in rural areas; and inadequate transportation systems. The distribution outlets are located mainly in major urban areas. The disadvantages are compounded because the sales outlets, if they are not part of the publisher's organizational setup, can return books that do not sell well.

Distribution in any business undertaking where products are intended for a large number of users must be well developed because it can mean the difference between success or failure of the enterprise. One of the main defects of book distribution in the Third World is the assumption that what is published will be sold. Curtis Benjamin, writing about indigenous publishing in Third World countries had this to say: "There is much more to the development of indigenous publishing than the availability of suitable facilities and materials and capital for the printing of books." In his estimation "far too many book-development programs had failed because they had concentrated on production and neglected distribution and utilization." He points out that "in too many cases, after thousands of desperately needed books had been produced, it was discovered that far too many copies were left sitting in warehouses—that there were no suitable mechanisms or facilities for effective movement of the books into the gaps where they were needed." Book gaps, he continues, cannot be filled by books alone—the supply of books, no matter how plentiful, will not fill a country's need unless adequate marketing mechanisms and sufficient distribution channels have been provided and unless rewarding use of the books is assured in the end.[6]

Roger Kirkpatrick's assessment of distribution is far more blunt and to the point. "Any book is dead until read, when it becomes alive," he writes, pointing out further that, "usually it is only read when bought. It is only bought if distributed from author through publisher to reader."[7] In his estimation a literate society is as dependent on its ability to distribute books widely as it is on the authors who write the books. No publishing industry can adequately serve a nation's needs without the support of a sound and efficient network of competent wholesalers and retailers. Yet in most developing countries little attention is given—even by publishers—to the essentiality of such a distribution system.

The difficulties of distribution are also formidable for publishers in industrialized countries. In a speech at the annual meeting of the

Book Manufacturers Institute in 1983, Brooks Thomas, president of Harper & Row, pointed out that rising costs could be attributed in part to an "inefficient distribution system" in the United States. Of course, this statement must be qualified by the context in which it was made. What is inefficient in the United States is different from what does not work in the Third World. Another example is Japan where, despite a very well-developed and unique distribution system, readers, served by over 4,000 publishers, 60 distributors, and 20,000 or more bookstores throughout the country, are sometimes neglected by the sophisticated automation of the system that is not geared to meet special requests outside the distribution pattern.[8] Keeping in perspective the overall state of publishing in Third World countries, it is not difficult to recognize the monumental tasks facing them. Even meeting the basic needs for achieving mass distribution, i.e., adequate book manufacturing equipment, distribution equipment, display equipment, a distribution system and plan (including transportation), necessary capital, an adequate editorial and production staff, and tax relief, is beyond the capabilities and capacities of publishers in most developing countries. Datus Smith has pointed out that even Third World countries capable of developing a satisfactory distribution system have to recognize the role of mass distribution in helping to develop an educated citizenry. Educators and decision makers, he shows, readily accept that the advancement of development depends on a well-developed educational system and a nationwide system of libraries. They fail, however to recognize that these must be supported by a nationwide system of distribution and sale of inexpensive books. A major reason for this flawed thinking, Smith opines, is that publishing, and particularly book distribution, is viewed as "just business" rather than part of the basic makeup of a country's educational system.[9]

Other Factors

The fault does not lie entirely with publishers in Third World countries. The problems of mass distribution are inevitably exacerbated by a combination of political, economic, resource, and organizational problems that are often beyond the control of local publishing enterprises. Even though the demand for books may exist on a large scale, the nature of local trading patterns and the prevalent bazaar-type economy may not be conducive to large-scale distribution of books. In addition, large bookstores in urban centers may concentrate on selling imported books or books in the languages of former colonial masters because of high profits from middle-class clientele. All these factors can lead to a chicken-egg syndrome that prevents publishers in Third World countries from increasing distribution: although production unit costs could be kept low with larger print runs, distribution problems limit the size of printings thereby resulting in high printing costs and ultimately high distribution costs. Distribution is also dependent upon the concentration of buyers in a location, the distance of outlet location from the source, demand for the product, and nature of the product. In many Third World countries, where populations are primarily rural and widely dispersed, prospective book buyers are difficult to reach. Even when they are accessible, however, their priorities are often necessities: food, clothing, medicine, and so on. Books are not foremost in their consideration.[10]

Each region, country, language or ethnic group has its particular problems affecting distribution. Still, there are some common difficulties. These are linked primarily to the sheer size of many Third World countries, which has implications for transportation and postal services, both of which are often poorly developed, unreliable, slow, and expensive. In addition there are a limited network of bookstores or other outlets, most of which are in large cities; few libraries, which are usually poorly stocked; and vast rural areas with few sales outlets and scattered populations with low purchasing power.

Many assessments of marketing strategies consider the problem primarily from the publishers' viewpoint of business, the government's position of policy and planning, or the scholars' empirical analysis approach. The cultural and social dimensions of the book buyer or reader are seldom studied.[11] However, these dimensions, which are dependent on local economic systems, cultural biases, and educational attainment, often determine effective approaches to distributing books in rural areas. Publishing systems in Third World countries have been invariably inherited from colonial masters. They almost always have continued to follow the operational patterns of industrialized countries, which often are not suited to the peculiarities of local conditions and, therefore, cannot adequately address local needs. Ideally, each Third World country should, on the basis of the universal principles of publishing as a business, develop its own approach to publishing as a cultural asset. This is seldom done. In recent years, there have been laudable efforts in a few countries to develop publishing that is more immediately adaptable and responsive to their situations. Publishers in Malaysia, India, Singapore, and Egypt, for example, have made great strides in tailoring local publishing, including distribution, to answer the particular needs of their citizens.

Asian Efforts

Even though the general picture of distribution in the Third World is the same everywhere, the actual situation varies with each country and region. In 1981, Asia, with a total population of over 2.6 billion inhabitants, accounted for about 20 percent of the total world production of 729,000 book titles. The industrialized world accounted for about 80 percent with only 25 percent of the world's population. There was an absolute increase in number of book titles produced in Asia from 1970 to 1981, from 75,000 to 147,000. However, population increases, from 2.09 billion in 1970 to 2.6 billion in 1981, reduced the number of titles produced per million inhabitants from 63 to 56 for the same years, respectively.[12] Of course, since the figures for Japan are also included here, the final total for the rest of Asia is much lower.

As more and more countries in Asia begin to recognize that education is fundamental to development, there is a parallel realization of the importance of publishing and, thereby, the need to improve distribution systems. There are, nevertheless, a number of obstacles. Among them, Abdul Hasan stresses, are the great number of languages within many countries, the lack of endogenous authorship, copyright problems, the lack of paper, the high cost of production, and the difficulties of promoting and maintaining the reading habit in rural areas where most of the population live.[13]

Some Asian countries have begun to develop networks of printing/publishing facilities in rural areas as a means of overcoming distribution problems. One such program is Indonesia's mobile printing *Micropu* units. By providing printing facilities to local communities, reading material produced by the people themselves is made available. Inevitably, this will enhance reader interest. This does not, however, solve the problem of getting a wider range of books to rural areas from the urban centers. Other efforts have concentrated directly on distribution solutions. There are mobile and community libraries in Korea, India, Thailand, and Pakistan. Home libraries, which have been vigorously promoted in Korea, are being considered by other countries in the region. There are also the traveling bookshops of the government publishing house Balai Pustaka that now reach twenty-six provinces in Indonesia. Balai Pustaka has also set up 2,453 library clubs in provincial cities. Following the lead of Korea, Thailand has organized a national book distribution center with twenty-nine participating publishers to help distribute books more widely throughout the country. China has a highly developed centralized distribution system which is run by the Xin Hua Book Store Agency with more than 5,000 retail outlets throughout the country.

Distribution in Asia is generally handled by wholesalers, retail bookstores, book clubs, and in a few instances kiosks, newspaper stands, and supermarkets. Libraries are responsible for the lending form of distribution. Although wholesalers are important for stimulating book circulation and are the main source of books for retailers, there are comparatively few wholesalers in Asia, particularly if one does not count those in Japan. This is still a new concept in the region. A few wholesalers exist in Korea, Malaysia, India, and Singapore. Hasan thinks that it will be "rather difficult to achieve a real breakthrough in book distribution in Asia without national wholesale distribution agencies." He feels that they could "act as a catalyst in the movement of books to every corner of a country."[14]

There are very few bookstores in most Asian countries and these are almost always concentrated in cities and large towns. They suffer from lack of ready credit and high overhead. In addition, publishers often bypass small bookstores to supply books directly to libraries and educational institutions. Many governments have not recognized the importance of publishing's role in development and its ability to enhance the country's intellectual level. Thus they tend to overlook the benefits publishing could derive from preferential treatment. This includes the role of bookstores in the distribution makeup.

With the exception of India, book clubs have not developed extensively in Asia despite the apparent advantages they would have in bringing books to a wider range of readers.

The future of distribution in Asia is bound to improve because many countries are more aware of the far-reaching implications of its advantages. This awareness has been cultivated and encouraged by subregional publishers organizations, national book councils, and two regionwide organizations that are linked with UNESCO: the Regional Book Development Center for Asia in Karachi, Pakistan, and the Asian Cultural Centre for UNESCO in Tokyo, Japan.

The Vastness of Africa's Problem

The vast continent of Africa, with 10 percent of the world's population, produced a meager 2 percent of the global output of books in 1981 or 14,000 titles in total.[15] William Moutchia, director of the Regional Center for Book Promotion in Africa South of the Sahara, characterizes Africa's book industry as young. Africa remains behind other parts of the world, he feels, because no colonial powers made a deliberate attempt to introduce education or publishing. "Publishing," he points out, "was accidental and occasional, with a religious objective"; religious missionaries set up the first rudimentary printing facilities to produce religious books and pamphlets. When the colonial powers left Africa many took the infrastructures of publishing with them. Comparatively speaking, Africa has achieved a lot because it started with nothing and developed something.[16]

Distribution, he admits, is still in dire straits, particularly because transportation systems are poor, government action is ineffectual, and interference is excessive. In one country, the ministry of education could not get needed syllabi to remote provinces because it had not devised an effective means of transporting the books. These books piled up in provincial educational offices but never reached the schools. Even now books prescribed by the ministry tend to reach their destinations after the exams have been given. Because they can no longer be used, the books then remain in booksellers' depots or in the provincial educational offices.

Since much of the distribution in Africa is concerned with educational books, the government usually handles it. The remainder is handled by trade outlets and, to a lesser extent, by church bookshops, pavement "bookshops" (bazaar type), and newspaper stands. A representative government distribution setup, the Kenya School Equipment Scheme, has been described by Henry Chakava. It supplies equipment to the nearly 10,000 primary schools. In 1977, 60 percent of the $5.5 million allotted to the scheme was spent on the purchase of books. After school book requirements from each school are approved, based on a list of titles drawn up by the Ministry of Education, tenders from publishers are received in the middle of the year, and finished supplies are available for delivery before the next school year begins. This ten-year-old arrangement is aimed at ensuring that book supplies reach rural areas on time and at reasonable cost to the government. Before the scheme came into effect, schools dealt directly with bookstores.[17]

The scheme, however, is not without its critics. Chakava stresses that it has led to the demise of many small rural bookstores. This, in turn, threatens a healthy and active book industry with bookstores as key distribution and marketing outlets. These bookstores played an essential role in the educational and cultural development of the country by providing, in addition to school books, general books which could help improve the reading habits of rural people. Among other difficulties, the transportation problem is a tremendous one because the scheme owns the trucks used for distribution, yet it does not have the know-how for using them efficiently or the manpower and expertise for their care and maintenance.

Kenyan distribution problems are representative of the situation throughout most of Africa. The trade outlets in Kenya are located mainly in the major cities and large towns. Nairobi has the largest number of outlets and the largest bookshop in the country, the Textbook Centre, which controls approximately 20 percent of the total book market. Other major outlets are also located in Kakamega, Kisumu Meru, Mombasa, Nakuru, and Nyeri.

The defunct East African Literature Bureau, which operated in Kenya, was instrumental in setting up a book access scheme for African readers, particularly in rural areas, which included establishing libraries, postal borrowing, and mobile book vans. The Kenya National Library Service has eleven branches throughout the country. In addition, seven mobile libraries travel throughout the remote areas. There are also city libraries, university libraries, and numerous school libraries with an average of 1,000 volumes each. In Chakava's estimation, libraries to most Kenyans symbolize the elite and are not used by ordinary citizens. Book clubs have been tried in the past, but not with much success. For example, Heinemann established a Spear Books/Joe Magazine Book Club in 1976, but this did not arouse much interest. Nor did the Textbook Centre's club, which offered mainly imported paperbacks. The lack of a functioning national book development council, although a council has been established in principle, is also hampering activities in Kenya.

Latin America: Potential but Little Power

Latin America, with 8.1 percent of the world's population in 1981, produced 5.2 percent of the global total of titles, giving it the greatest number of titles per million inhabitants among the developing regions.[18]

Most of the large-scale publishing is concentrated, however, in Argentina, Brazil, and Mexico, with Colombia, Chile, Cuba, Peru, Uruguay, and Venezuela publishing on a smaller but adequate scale.

Alberto E. Augsburger points out that, as in the other developing regions, Latin America's main publishing problems are caused by illiteracy, with about 75 percent of all illiterates living in rural areas, and the lack of adequate marketing and distribution facilities. At present the following types of book distributors exist in the region: (1) *nonexclusive*—works with a number of publishers, usually not more than ten, on exclusive or nonexclusive basis; (2) *exclusive*—deals with one publisher; (3) *dependent*—branch office or warehouse of foreign publisher; (4) *combined*—deals with some books in addition to main line of newspapers and magazines; (5) *occasional*—sporadic transaction; and (6) *specialized*—specialized books.[19]

In many Latin American countries a publisher may have to have several arrangements for distribution. In addition to distributors there are outlets that sell books as well as other types of merchandise—such as supermarkets, drugstores, or stationery stores—and there are traditional bookstores. This has some implications for the role of traditional booksellers in the intellectual and cultural milieu, for the competition of the marketplace often forces them to concentrate on the stocking of "popular" books. Other channels of distribution include kiosks, schools, house-to-house sales, libraries, mail-order sales, and book clubs.

The problems of distribution in Latin America are ostensibly not as complicated as in other Third World regions, mainly because Spanish is spoken in most Latin American countries. The movement of books across borders, particularly from larger publishing nations such as Argentina, Chile, or Mexico to nearby countries, should, theoretically, be simple. The realities of governmental restrictions, however, are one impediment. Tax barriers, customs laws, cultural protectionism, and political pressures restrict the free flow of books into and out of a country and, inevitably, throughout a country. The difficulties in distributing books across national borders explains, in part, why Latin America produces the highest number of book titles produced per million inhabitants in the Third World.

A 1974 seminar in Costa Rica, "The Role of the Book in Change Process in Latin America," highlighted some of the difficulties faced by publishers. One finding was that there is no communication among Latin American publishers. Many do not know what their counterparts in other countries are producing. This failure in communication, says Helbert Guevara Mayorga, is one reason for a decreased demand for books in the region. Another finding was that low productivity hampered large-scale production. Other problems mentioned at the conference included inadequate marketing infrastructures, monetary problems hindering free trade between countries, small editions of titles, and increased costs and higher prices.[20]

It is estimated that by the year 2000, when over 600 million Latin Americans will require a more advanced educational system, books will have to play a more active role. Mayorga reported that looking toward this eventuality, a number of steps have been taken. "In September 1969, for example, the 'Experts' Meeting for Increasing Book Production in Latin America was held in Bogota, Colombia, under the auspices of UNESCO, attended by representatives from the entire area, and from which emerged positive results."[21] One result was the creation of the Bogota-based CERLAL (Regional Center for the Promotion of Books in Latin America) to study publishing problems of the region. In November 1971 it held the first course on Latin American editorial and production administration, stressing the importance of books in economic development. The Regional Office of Central America and Panama (ROCAP) was created by the Organization of Central American States (ODECA) for the purpose of printing school books for the area. "Although this experiment has not lived up completely to expectations due to local idiosyncrasies," Mayorga says, "a great gap has been filled with the publication of millions of textbooks that are already being used throughout the area. These books, printed in large runs and exempted from taxation, are very valuable material produced at low costs."[22]

What Does It Mean?

The problems of distribution are generally the same in almost all Third World countries: illiteracy, large rural populations far from publishing centers, lack of professional know-how, inadequate transportation or postal systems, government publishing competing with commercial publishing, and low print runs of titles. At the same time, distribution is subject to the influences of each locale whether it be a large urban bookstore in Nairobi, a small bookshop in rural Indonesia, or a provincial government distribution center somewhere in Latin America. A. A. Read points out some of the major distribution problems unique to developing countries: "woefully inadequate" storage facilities that expose book stocks to physical damage and pilferage; inadequate transportation systems that cause loss, damage and delay; and inadequate trade outlets.[23]

The elements that constitute the distribution mix include textbooks as a mainstay, newspapers and magazines as bread-and-butter items, and, where available, general books, scholarly books, and reference books. The role of textbooks in distribution, and in publishing in the Third World in general, is overwhelming. As Curtis Benjamin notes, the market for educational books is almost "everywhere not only the largest but also the most profitable" for indigenous book publishers.[24] Textbooks occupy a place of primacy in a nations' cultural development because they serve educational needs and provide potential markets for Third World publishers. The development of this market is of vital importance in the development of a book industry, especially if the industry can also be geared to provide general books to the public. In order to develop an effective market demand, the educational system must, of course, be organized to encourage the use of books as basic tools of instruction and to instill lifetime reading habits in students. The book component must be carefully planned and integrated into the total educational system.

This demand for books is one factor that has a profound impact on distribution because what is not sought will not be bought. Another factor is level of literacy. The rate of literacy will be high if the educational system is well set up and encourages reading beyond school requirements and beyond school completion. This will in turn contribute to a high demand for books and will help keep the distribution process in high gear. Continual and well-developed distribution, based on an adequate selection of book titles, will, in turn, support a high literacy rate. Naturally, all of the foregoing will take an opposite turn if the educational structure does not contribute to improving literacy in a country.

The publishing process is already somewhat hampered by the nature of its products; a nonstandardized commodity that changes and must be reevaluated each time a new version appears. Unlike products such as clothing or food which can be produced in vast quantities in the same mold or model, books are *always* different. The normal process of supply and demand that exists for the average commercial enterprise does not exist for publishing because the product is constantly changing. Thus conditioning the buyer to accept the product *before* it is actually produced is a crucial facet in the publishing process.

Book reading has economic, cultural, social, and educational implications. Once the buyer accepts books as enhancing each of these aspects of life, he will be receptive to book buying. If this can be accomplished on a nationwide scale, book sales and distribution will improve.

What Direction for Distribution?

The direction is obvious. The problem is: can Third World countries make the turn? All evidence indicates that there will be a tremendous increase in educational needs, both qualitative and quantitative. Increased populations will put a strain on outmoded educational systems and on the mechanisms that support them, particularly culture awareness, development, and books. Or will it be books? We are not certain of the continued role of books in light of new electronic information techniques that are becoming available. The scope of education expansion was described in an article by Christina Barbin in *Development Forum* in which she says that "between 1960 and 1980, the rate of school attendance in secondary education in Africa quadrupled. In 15 countries, over 70 percent of all children between the ages of 6 and 11 attend school. . . . At the same time, illiteracy among adults has substantially declined."[25] Datus Smith also recognized, however, that in spite of the increasing availability of education "book-publishing [had] not kept up with [this momentum]."[26]

Alvin Toffler describing the next major economic-social revolution, what he calls the Third Wave, for humankind, says that "it [will make] us look at education . . . with fresh eyes. . . . All our conventional assumptions about education need to be re-examined both in the rich countries and the poor."[27] He asks telling questions, which have also been asked by education experts, about the meaning of literacy in light of new communications technologies which may make reading unnecessary for illiterate people in Third World countries. He quotes specialists who question the need to know how to write in the face of upcoming advancements in communications and those who feel that a return to oral traditions may benefit some societies.

Another study by Ithiel de Sola Pool confirmed that society is "in the middle of an information explosion" that is changing the pattern of human work endeavors.[28] The amount of information that is being produced is increasing at a tremendous rate, but the amount actually being consumed is not keeping pace. This is causing information overload and a decline in productivity of print media—although there is an actual increase, in absolute terms, of words produced. The shift away from print media to nonprint media particularly exacerbates the trend toward lesser consumption.

These phenomena are being looked at in industrialized nations which have, or are developing, the capacity to cope with the trend. What of the Third World countries that are only now beginning to find their way through the maze of educational needs facing them? How will they manage to use the rapid advancements in technologies and educational techniques while trying to balance their meager and often dwindling resources with their overwhelmingly large needs?

Some information has been given here and many questions posed. The formulation of answers is not easy because real analysis is not possible. Statistics to do in-depth studies are often not available. This chapter has attempted to pull together existing research; it does not guarantee solutions. One thing is clear: most Third World publishing sprang from and continues to emulate the systems inherited from industrialized countries. Studying local conditions might suggest mechanisms for improving distribution in each country. Eduard Kimman's study on Indonesian publishing, which looks at the economic setup throughout the country, is an example of this approach.[29] The reality is that the Third World, having done much to develop publishing from the editorial, design, and production aspects, must now improve distribution. Whether the communications revolution is around the corner or not, existing publishers, expectant readers and buyers, and educational planners need the tools that are available now. These are books, and moving books from producer to buyer means distribution. Book development programs have tended to neglect distribution in favor of editing and production. The conclusions are clear, for as Roger Kirkpatrick lamented "there is now a very real danger that as society develops those who publish and distribute books will lose the race to match the greatly stimulated expectations of immediate availability."[30]

Notes

This chapter is an extended version of an article written for my column "Writing about Books," "Distribution: The Neglected factor," *Asian Book Development* 14, no. 4 (1983).

[1] M. Lee, *Bookmaking* (New York: R. R. Bowker, 1979), 10.
[2] Ibid., 10.
[3] Ibid., 11.
[4] Ibid.
[5] Ibid.
[6] C. G. Benjamin, *A Candid Critique of Book Publishing* (New York: R. R. Bowker, 1977), 120.
[7] R. Kirkpatrick, "Distribution—General," in P. Oakeshott and C. Bradley, eds., *The Future of the Book—Part 1. The Impact of New Technologies* (Paris: UNESCO, 1982), 57.
[8] H. R. Lottman, "The Distribution Dilemmas," *Publishers Weekly*, October 1, 1978.
[9] D. C. Smith, Jr., *A Guide to Book Publishing* (New York: R. R. Bowker, 1966), 15.
[10] A. A. Arboleda, "A Giant Step In Tokyo," in S. Minowa and A. A. Arboleda, eds., *Scholarly Publishing in Asia, Proceedings of the Conference of University Presses in Asia and the Pacific Area* (Tokyo: University of Tokyo Press, 1973).
[11] A. A. Arboleda, "English Language Scholarly Publishing in Japan," *Scholarly Publishing* 6, no. 3 (1975).
[12] UNESCO, *Statistical Yearbook* (Paris: UNESCO, 1983).
[13] A. Hasan, *Promoting National Strategies in Asia and the Pacific: Problems and Prospectives* (Paris: UNESCO, 1981), 19.
[14] Ibid., 20.
[15] UNESCO, *Statistical Yearbook*, 1983.
[16] William Moutchia, interview in *Asian Book Development* 13, no. 4 (1982).
[17] Henry Chakava, *Books and Reading in Kenya* (Paris: UNESCO, 1982), 21-22.
[18] UNESCO, *Statistical Yearbook*, 1983.
[19] A. E. Augsburger, *The Latin American Book Market: Problems and Prospects* (Paris: UNESCO, 1982), 61-62.
[20] H. G. Mayorga, "Publishing in Latin America: Present Status," in S. Minowa, A. A. Arboleda, and N. Raj, eds., *International Scholarly Publishing, Proceedings of the Second International Conference on Scholarly Publishing* (Tokyo: University of Tokyo Press, 1976).
[21] Ibid., 39.
[22] Ibid., 40.

[23] A. A. Read, "Problems of International Book Distribution," in P. Oakeshott and C. Bradley, eds., *The Future of the Book—Part I: The Impact of New Technologies* (Paris: UNESCO, 1982), 76.

[24] Benjamin, *Candid Critique*, 122.

[25] C. Barbin, "Present and Future," *Development Forum*, 11, no. 3 (1983).

[26] Smith, *Guide to Book Publishing*, 150.

[27] A. Toffler, *The Third Wave* (New York: Willilam Morrow, 1980).

[28] I. de Sola Pool, "Tracking the Flow of Information," *Science* 221, no. 4461 (1983).

[29] E. Kimman, *Indonesian Publishing: Economic Organizations in a Langganan Society* (Baarn, Netherlands: Hollandia, 1981).

[30] Kirkpatrick, "Distribution," 55.

6

Educational Publishing and Book Provision

Pernille Askerud

In poor countries, with untrained teachers, the textbook becomes the most important, if not the only, vehicle for the curriculum. Without the textbook, skills, concepts and content required by the curriculum cannot be taught. In the absence of any other widely available sources of information, the textbook also becomes the most important and often the only source of content and pedagogic information for the teacher. Furthermore, since often neither pupils nor teachers have access to alternative materials, the textbook also becomes the sole basis for examination and assessment. Many countries in Asia base important school leaving and school promotion examinations entirely on textual recall from an established and prescribed textbook. The textbook thus assumes far wider importance in poorer countries than in more developed countries where there is a wider variety and availability of alternative materials, viewpoints and sources.[1]

Since textbooks and other instructional materials have a direct impact on what is taught in schools and how it is taught, curriculum development and curriculum materials are sensitive matters which are of great political importance. This is why the book sector in industrialized countries receives both direct and indirect subsidies. There is always a need for a mechanism to review and control the quality of learning materials used in classrooms with regard to relevance, content, educational approach and efficacy, as well as to ensure that the provision of learning materials reflects government policies.

The implementation of policies regarding the content and quality of education, equity and the adoption of low-cost strategies for the development and production of instructional materials starts here. While there is no single way of improving the provision of basic learning materials, there are many possible solutions, according to the different level of development reached.

The provision of basic learning materials differs from one country to another, and various approaches are used. While some countries struggle to establish mechanisms for the production of relevant curriculum materials, others focus on issues of institutional sustainability and the role of the government. While some donors recommend the withdrawal of the public sector from the production of basic learning materials, others supply gifts of books or support the establishment or expansion of government presses.

This diversity shows how complex the issue is and indicates the difficulties that face planners of basic education programs. The problems are of two kinds: those that are related to content, presentation, use and provision, and those related to the technical and financial aspects of production, distribution and funding.

The strategies and policies adopted by a government to meet the demand for textbooks and other instructional materials should be determined by a national policy for the provision of instructional materials for schools and nonformal programs. This policy is an integral part of a wider national book policy. The educational planner must consider each of the following aspects of book provision separately as well as how they affect each other. The majority of these issues are greatly influenced by national policies or the lack of them.

- goals, both medium- and long-term, for the provision of learning materials at various levels of education;
- policy issues: language(s) of instruction, curricula, access, level of provision at various levels of education, economy and involvement of the private sector;
- educational issues: curricula and text development (issues of content, relevance, educational approach, media and presentation), teacher training, needs assessment and integration of examination requirements;
- planning, management and monitoring of the process: who and how, and modalities and delegation of responsibility;
- economic sustainability: means of funding and cost recovery, the role of the private sector, affordability and economic sustainability;
- industrial/technical issues: development, production and distribution (sale) of learning materials;
- technical sustainability: research, renewal, information, training and needs assessment;
- skills development: curriculum developers, writers, illus-

trators, designers, typesetters, printers, teachers and distributors;
- reading environment: availability of supplementary reading materials in libraries and in the market, and the general economy, purchase ability and affordability;
- legal aspects: copyright and other international instruments, such as the Florence Agreement and its Protocol; local legislation concerning educational publishing.

The differences between general publishing and the development and production of textbooks arise from the role government plays in the following areas of production: the initiative in publishing and the development of materials; funding, budgeting and cost-effectiveness; and distribution and teacher support. Textbook development and provision are complex issues that require compromise to meet objectives and cooperation between very different disciplines. A number of additional stages of testing and correction are required in the development of a good textbook that are not needed when developing a text such as a novel. The main difference is that the government and not the publisher makes most of the decisions.

The Role of the State in Educational Publishing

The biggest difference between general publishing and educational publishing is to be found in the state's dual and, possibly, conflicting roles as "author/publisher" and "customer." Various options for government intervention in relation to textbook production and book provision will now be considered. The provision of books for schools and nonformal education programs demands books and other instructional materials for the achievement of a certain level of educational attainment. The publishing initiative rests with the state and is guided by government policies for educational achievement, not by normal economic market forces. In other words, through its educational policies, the government decides how many and what books are needed in schools and how these books are paid for. There is no danger that books will not be sold.

In contrast, a publisher estimates the viability of a specific market, not only on the basis of market research into the demand for different kinds of books and the costs involved in their production and distribution, but also according to the level of professional competence and industrial development as well as the regulations and conditions of trade and the import and export of various items.

In many developing countries, most private sector publishers have not provided the conditions necessary for greater investment. There are many factors that may contribute to this. First, there is insufficient demand for books, newsprint and other printed materials; second, people cannot afford to buy books; third, there is no cost-effective distribution system in place; fourth, imported paper is too expensive for efficient printing; fifth, lack of skilled publishing personnel; and, finally, there are no opportunities to become involved in the production of learning materials—the only kind of books that have an assured market.

These factors also explain why so many textbook projects have had so little impact in developing countries. A successful program for the provision of learning materials and the economic conditions that allow a market-oriented publishing sector to develop are interdependent. The state must create favorable conditions for a local book industry to develop.

The size of the task of providing books and the economic opportunities that are opened also produce problems. To balance equity and the economy requires considerable resources that cannot be paid for in the foreseeable future. It also requires ingenuity to overcome the inherent contradiction between a noncommercial and commercial strategy by the development of objectives that seem almost irreconcilable. For this reason, it is difficult to consider that the provision of books can be achieved and maintained without government direction and intervention. The success of the undertaking is, ultimately, a question of policy, political will, and the resources needed to support the policy. Cooperation between public- and private-sector publishing in textbook development and provision allows for many options or combinations as illustrated in Table 1.

One strategy is to develop the necessary skills and capacity in the public sector for the production and distribution of instructional materials. This has been the common practice in developing countries in the last twenty years. The negative effect of this strategy on the development of alternative publishing initiatives is substantial and it may unintentionally have slowed book development in developing countries.

When faced with the problem of insufficient funding to meet the demand for learning materials, many governments tried to solve the problem by reducing the cost of book provision. This was done either through developing domestic facilities for the production of learning materials in an attempt to eliminate the profit element or by importing low-cost materials from abroad.[2] In many developing countries, the government did not have the choice of subcontracting work to private-sector publishing, since the local capacity was insufficient to do the work, and so was obliged to start publishing enterprises. As shown in book-sector studies and reviews of the national provision of learning materials, this approach has not proved successful either in terms of economy or quality.

Table 1. Government/Private Sector Distribution of Responsibilities

	Alternative					
	1	2	3	4	5	6
Curriculum	0	0	0	0	0	0
Elaboration of texts and illustrations	0	0	0	0	X	X
Editing	0	0	0	X	X	X
Prepress preparation	0	0	0	X	X	X
Printing and binding	0	X	X	0	X	X
Distribution, storage, sale	0	0	X	0	0	X

Note: 0 = government undertaking; X = private-sector undertaking

When the state monopolizes the instructional materials market, it prevents the development and growth of both local publishing and a commercial market for book sales. Unless the government undertakes to produce and sell a wide variety of books and other printed materials needed to maintain literacy, there will be no indigenous materials for people to read once they have left school. The absence of private-sector publishing also affects the market for imported books and printed materials because multinational publishers need sales outlets, such as a network of bookshops. It is unlikely that multinational publishers would be ready to establish a separate distribution network in a country that does not already have a commercial distribution network for books.

When the state controls textbook production, the level of professionalism can vary because production occurs according to the administrative procedures of a civil service. Staff development and promotion obey civil service practices and this can fail to meet professional standards. Rules and regulations for purchasing and subcontracting developed for the civil service are generally unsuited to a commercially competitive publishing house. The costs of producing the materials and the maintenance of equipment become unclear. A major problem for state enterprises is that they often have no working capital but depend on a wide range of subsidies for the necessary maintenance or expenditure on consumables and machinery. Forward planning is very difficult in such circumstances, and this makes production highly uneconomic.

Another strategy—and probably a more cost-effective one—is to create conditions (for example, through legislation and tax incentives) that encourage the involvement of private-sector publishing in the production of learning materials.

The problem of achieving technical and economic sustainability, and a lack of sufficient and recurrent funding to produce and distribute quality materials in sufficient quantities, are common in many developing countries. The recommendations made by various studies regarding this problem indicate that a greater involvement of the private sector both as producers and buyers may provide a solution. The involvement of the private sector in production breaks the monopoly that many state enterprises have exerted and opens up opportunities for general publishing, which may lead to a higher level of book awareness. There is a trend in more recent projects for the government to play a coordinating and monitoring role in the institutions that write, produce, distribute and market books, while production and distribution is subcontracted to the private sector.

This strategy leaves the government to deal with what it does best, that is, to decide educational policies, make laws and regulations, and exercise quality control—in other words, to carry out the planning, management and supervision of the implementation of government policies in education.

A third strategy is for state publishing units to be owned by the government but to operate as fully commercial publishing companies, which bid for work along with private publishing companies. The costs are then clear. In this way, the state acts as a motor for book development, such as through the development of a distribution system for books and through skills development. It also ensures that books that commercial companies cannot, or will not, publish are still published—for example, books for use in schools in small indigenous languages.

The only way to guarantee that both educational requirements and considerations of cost-effectiveness are satisfied is to develop a coherent system for the provision of instructional materials that covers the whole process from the development of the materials to their distribution and quality control.

This system is expressed in comprehensive national book policies and in a specific policy for the provision of learning materials for the educational sector. The formulation of and adherence to such policies are the most important functions and responsibilities of the government.

Planning, Management, and Quality Control

Government policies and school conditions differ. Planning for the wide range of materials needed for education must, however, always be based on the conditions that obtain and on realistic calculations. Surveys of conditions and a thorough needs assessment, along with a careful scrutiny of the relevance and usefulness of existing materials, should be undertaken periodically. On the basis of the information obtained, a plan for book provision can be drawn up. As curriculum changes take time to implement, plans should cover a period of several years.

It is possible to make good use of available resources by means of inventiveness and realistic planning. Realistic planning also means that not all solutions can be applied everywhere, not even in the same country. Situations and conditions vary, and so must strategies if an economic and effective system for book provision is to be developed.

In many places, costs of production and distribution would be cut if books were lent to students and used by more than one. This demands that the books be of a certain quality. If, on the other hand, there are no places in homes where schoolchildren can keep and work with books without damaging them, this is not necessarily a desirable solution. If could, however, work if the students were made to keep the books at the school and only use them there, in which case the provision of storage facilities in the school would be a necessary part of the book provision program.[3]

It is almost impossible to achieve an economy that makes it possible for the publishing industry to prosper without policies for book development and book provision. To be effective, such policies must be based on accurate and extensive information concerning book provision. This also means that there may be variations in how the demands for learning materials are met in different parts of the country.

A government can undertake more or fewer activities, but even when it delegates tasks to subcontractors, the overall responsibility for the timely and satisfactory provision of good quality instructional materials should remain with the government. To be able to assume this responsibility, staff dealing with these issues must be adequately trained to plan, manage, supervise and control the work.

In addition, the government must exercise quality control in terms of content, presentation and appearance. For example, the quality of the binding and the specifications for the paper used for the inside pages and the book cover are important because they determine the life of the book. Once there is no cover or the book starts to fall apart due to poor binding, its life expectancy is reduced. Too often, books used in schools and educational programs are so cheaply and poorly produced that they disintegrate in the first week of use.

While the most expensive solution is not necessarily the best, the cheapest solution is often not cost-effective. When tenders are called for textbook production it is important that those who commission the work are capable of judging the quality of the content and of specifying the quality of paper, print, cover, and binding needed to achieve the most cost-effective product.

The collection of learning materials in support of the curriculum depends largely on government policies. Should books for the education sector be original creations, adaptations, or translations of available titles or be procured from available national and international titles? Many economic and educational factors must be taken into consideration before a decision can be made.

The development of individual titles follows the publication of curriculum guidelines. The question is whether the development of texts should be done by people working within the ministry of education or by private-sector publishers? Likewise, should production be undertaken by the public sector or by the private sector or by a combination of the two?

A central issue for curriculum development units in ministries of education all over the world is how to transform a curriculum into educationally sound materials. The writing and design of educational materials require more than knowledge of a subject. To know how to write and to present a subject so that the book will be an effective educational tool requires knowledge and experience as well as a sense of book design. Writing and designing successfully for children are not the same thing as writing for adults.

Finally, field testing, evaluation, and revision of the materials must be done regularly.

Not by Textbooks Alone

The learning materials required to help the teacher are not just textbooks. The availability of textbooks has long been recognized as an important factor in educational attainment, and governments and agencies have, to the exclusion of other aspects of the problem, focused on projects and programs for textbook provision. However, books other than textbooks and instructional materials that are not books (such as boards and chalk, maps and flip charts, scissors, pencils, notebooks and writing pads, equipment and tools needed for science instruction, radio and television, computers and so on), are equally important for improving educational achievement. The choice of cost-effective materials varies and depends on many factors.

Educational achievement is determined by the teacher's knowledge of the subject and pedagogical skills, the availability of textbooks and other learning materials, and the time spent by pupils in learning. The levels and range of instructional materials available to teachers and students determine what goes on in a classroom. Where there is money for books and other learning materials, teachers are, in general, better qualified and the tuition provided is more diversified and more efficient than it is when there are few textbooks and when the teachers have no greater access to supplementary reading materials than do their students.

But when textbooks are available, the importance of training teachers in the use of new curriculum materials must not be ignored. The effectiveness of whatever learning materials are available depends on the ability of the teacher to use them as intended. Any efficient curriculum and textbook development program should include the development of teachers' manuals and additional teaching materials, and these materials should be introduced to the teachers by means of inservice training courses.

The scarcity of educational materials is a problem because of a shortage of copies of textbooks and the small range of those available. Students do not learn at the same pace. The poor quality and uneven development of instructional materials for different levels of learning increase the teachers' difficulties in teaching. Different approaches require different learning materials. Double-shift and multigrade classrooms, for example, require more instructional materials than single-grade classrooms do.

In poor countries where books are scarce and teachers are often untrained, textbooks assume wider importance than they do in more developed countries. Then the textbook becomes the most important, if not the only means of teaching. Without the textbook, the skills, concepts, and content required by the curriculum cannot be taught. In the absence of other sources of information, the textbook becomes the most important and often the only source of content for the teacher and the sole basis for testing and assessment. The importance of textbooks when teachers are untrained is illustrated in a study[4] made in northeastern Brazil, in which the teachers were asked to sit a general, multidisciplinary examination with their students. The students did better than the teachers, which is explained by the fact that the students had learned more from their textbooks than from what the teachers had taught them.

The role played by textbooks in the education process needs to be evaluated with regard to financial, social, and cultural conditions. If textbook provision schemes originally developed to suit formal education programs do not correspond to the economic, social, and cultural realities of a developing country, then it may be more realistic to revise the concept of the textbook, not just the text itself. More research is needed into the relevance and effectiveness of learning materials in a particular context and into the effectiveness of simple guides, lesson plans, and workbooks. The interaction of examination requirements and other aspects of the learning process needs to be given more attention. In many classrooms, the examination requirements, not the syllabus, determine what is taught.

Where textbooks are scarce or available only when the student is at school, alternative forms of instructional materials may be more important and more effective. In cases where there are few books in schools and where the financial realities are such that only limited funds are available for learning materials, the most cost-effective teaching aid may be teachers' workbooks based on the curriculum.

Textbook content and the educational approach also need to be considered. In spite of the gains made in the development of curriculum materials, much more needs to be done. The content of instructional material needs to be seen as an ongoing activity. In general, curriculum materials are oriented toward people who live in cities, with a bias toward the norms and values of the often conservative upper classes of society. Educational materials, in more ways than one, often speak a language different from that of the students. Readability and presentation are important. Poor presentation and inappropriate levels of reading difficulty can mean that an otherwise good textbook fails in its purpose.

Basic Learning Materials: What Are They?

Textbooks are considered here as generic for all basic learning materials. Likewise, "book development" is a term that refers to the development not only of books but also many other printed and nonprinted information media. "Basic learning materials" refers to textbooks, other reading materials, equipment and tools used for instruction in the first level of education, such as chalkboards, maps, scissors, and simple science equipment as well as nondurable supplies used by the pupil and teacher, such as notebooks, pencils, and chalk.

Today, the learning materials used to support teaching cover a wide range of media. Besides books, audiovisual facilities, scientific and technical equipment, and computers have become an integral part of educational practice. At the 1996 Book Fair in Frankfurt, electronic publishing took up an entire hall. Some publishers estimate that, by the year 2000, electronic publishing could account for almost 40 percent of the industry's turnover. Most electronic publishing will be in the fields of education and reference books.

Not all teaching aids, however, are costly or require advanced technology. Learning aids other than textbooks have attracted little attention, though they do have an impact on the quality of the teaching in classrooms. In textbook projects, the focus has been on textbooks to the exclusion of other learning materials. The importance of other learning materials must be stressed.[5] However, the reality in many developing countries is that there are very few instructional materials available in classrooms. Some schools do not even have blackboards.

One of the most important suggestions made here is that successful planning for book provision must be based on what is realistic rather than on models imported from countries with different economic and social conditions. Whatever the effectiveness or quality of educational materials, no increase in the quality of instruction can be expected unless such materials are used and in quantity. If the conditions needed to achieve this are not provided, two systems will exist, neither of which is used effectively in teaching, and the result will be an increase in expenditure without a substantial improvement in effectiveness. The use of more traditional educational practices will, in certain situations, prove more economical, easier to sustain, and more effective.

To use the resources spent on educational materials effectively, inventiveness and flexibility are essential. A book such as *The Teacher's Handbook: Using the Local Environment*[6] illustrates how the quality of tuition can be significantly improved by using resources that are readily available in the local environment. Such resources cannot be a substitute for books, but they can supplement them and bring a relevance into teaching.

The need to focus on the local environment cannot be overstated. Children are born and brought up in a particular environment and by the time they go to school they have gained a great deal of experience from their local background. Linking what they need to learn to what they have already experienced can greatly facilitate their mastery of different subjects. Furthermore, the local environment has resources the teacher needs for teaching and for the preparation of learning aids. Such aids will enhance the effectiveness of the teacher.

Funding

The provision and production of instructional materials are particularly complicated because the usual economic considerations, notably the existence of a market, are invalid. Demand is determined by government policies when it comes to textbooks and other educational materials, and the money to pay for books comes from scare government resources. The greatest difference between general publishing and publishing for educational programs is in the area of finance.

Growth in the demand for services and a lack of funds pose serious problems for ministries of education almost everywhere. The expansion of the education sector has not been matched by an increase in the public financial resources available for it. In many developing countries, education commands a smaller budget in relative terms today than ever before. Today no developing country allocates more than 1 percent of its primary education budget for the purchase of textbooks.

An increase on average of one or two percentage points would ensure that the Organisation for Economic Cooperation and Development standards for book provision are met.

Though financial constraints are the most quoted cause for the failure to supply books in sufficient quantities, this may not be the only reason. It is true that a national system for book provision offers considerable economic opportunities for private-sector publishing. Many publishers in the industrialized countries wish to become involved in book provision in developing countries to make up for declining sales in their home markets. But things are different from the point of view of a national government.

Educational planners face many of the same problems as people who plan to introduce information technology. In both cases, the identification in fiscal terms of the cost and return of investments, based on traditional cost-benefit analysis, is almost impossible. What is the economic benefit of raising a society from illiteracy and creating a better informed and more competitive society?[7] And what are the costs involved?

Traditional concepts of cost-benefit analysis must be revised to reflect the interests involved. By expanding the concept of benefit to the broader one of "value" to encompass cost reduction and revenue production, and by the development of a private publishing sector and related industries, a more realistic model for the benefits of book development, including an improved quality of life, competitive advantage and the achievement of development goals, is provided.

Similarly, strategic planning for the provision of basic learning materials must be viewed as part of a much wider strategy for creating reading societies in developing countries. The promotion of educational publishing is probably the cheapest and most efficient way of ensuring that developing countries have access to information in a world where information has become one of the highest-valued currencies.

The failure to sustain the advances in educational publishing made by so many curriculum development projects is partly caused by the isolation of curriculum materials from the bulk of the rest of publishing, which is partly the result of a lack of long-term planning for book provision.

Private-sector enterprise cannot risk investments where there are no firmly established government policies that recognize the importance of books for development. Externally funded projects are not likely to commit funds to the building up of the necessary infrastructure—such as the development of an economic and efficient distribution system or storage facilities for books—in the absence of established policies and planning. External donors find it easier to justify their support for such activities when national policies determine the design of projects, decide the type of funding mechanisms to be used for external assistance, and outline the long-term strategy for the book sector.

Financial problems affect the entire process of book provision. A system is needed that is both affordable and sustainable. The issue of finance is related to long-term success more than anything else and the central policy is the means of dealing with it. There are basically three options for financing the supply of learning materials: free provision, subsidized provision, or commercial sale. Together, they allow for many combinations.

The adoption of a policy of equal access to education for all has made the free distribution of textbooks and instructional aids a logical approach for many developing countries. It has proved to be a policy that very few developing countries are able and willing to afford.

Though curriculum materials have increasingly been better designed, few countries have been able to meet the recurrent costs successfully. Many externally funded curriculum and book development projects have failed.

The difficulties in providing recurrent funding for production and distribution pose serious obstacles to the provision of basic learning materials. Many consider this to be the most serious problem.[8]

It is argued here that the problem of recurrent funding cannot be solved unless book provision is planned within the wider context of book development.

The provision of free instructional materials for primary school pupils has become policy in many developing countries. While the policy of providing free school books is widespread for the primary level of education, it is less common for other levels of education. In some respects, ministries of education are faced with fewer problems in the area of book provision at the secondary and tertiary levels of education, for no other reason than because students in this group are fewer in number and economically more privileged and because considerations of the language of instruction pose fewer problems with regard to textbooks than is the case in primary education. However, many of the problems now associated with the primary level will recur as enrollments in secondary education go up. A gap in the funding of secondary school textbooks and secondary school libraries is beginning to emerge in developing countries.

Affordability and Cost Recovery

A key area in systems of textbook provision is exactly who decides how to spend the available funds for books. As a general principle, the further this decision-making process is from the actual user of the material, the less efficiently the funds are used. It is interesting to note that where parents themselves, through a school association, control the use of funds (contributed by them) purchasing tends to be well organized and efficient.[9]

Although expenditure on textbooks represents only a small fraction of the annual recurrent costs in education, it does provide an opportunity for cost recovery. Consequently, many recent textbook projects have sought to transfer the costs from the government to parents, with a reduction in direct government involvement and a transfer of production to the private sector, which subsidizes the consumers rather than the producers.

Government subsidies can be either direct or indirect. Sometimes it is difficult to penetrate a system and to recognize all inputs made by the government. Generally, producer subsidies lead to a protected and noncompetitive market, and do not reduce inequalities. Subsidies to the consumer, on the other hand, allow for greater competition among producers of books and can be given on a discriminatory basis—books may be provided free to poor students.

Affordability at acceptable price levels becomes important when the cost of provision is transferred to the parents. Affordability is a complex issue. What parents can afford varies widely and any reduction in costs remains ineffective if it does not, in fact, achieve affordability for the buyers.

Affordability relates to the class of the purchasers, what languages they speak, and whether they are rural or urban dwellers. Affordability must depend on the total cost of providing the set of books needed to follow tuition at a certain level and not on the price of the individual book. Willingness to spend money on books depends on the level of book awareness and the general appreciation of education. To establish the various degrees of affordability market research must be undertaken.

A concept of affordability and the establishment of affordable levels of support from government and/or parents is an absolute parameter on publishing design and economics, and yet the affordability issue must be correctly identified and solved. In one country, a textbook project succeeded in reducing the cost of textbooks to parents by almost a half, and yet sales hardly changed at all. Although cost reduction had been achieved, it was not being lowered to the point where the majority of the parents could participate. Reduction of cost had merely made the books cheaper for the elitist group of parents who had always been able to afford to buy books.[10]

The issue of cost-effectiveness is closely related to affordability. In parent-purchase systems, a choice frequently exists between providing books of a very low quality to keep prices down and providing books at prices that only an elite can afford. When the government provides the books free of charge, this problem is avoided.

Book rental schemes and the establishment of revolving funds for the provision of books have been tried out by textbook projects in order to deal with some of these problems. For rental schemes to work, durable books must be printed. Books produced to last longer reduce costs by reducing the need for distribution. High production standards encourage the sale of secondhand books or the passing on of used books and so reduce the overall cost of book provision. It is more economic in the long run to raise the quality of the books produced than to reduce production costs to a bare minimum.

Book rental schemes have been difficult to manage. They require staff trained to handle money, manage stock, and supervise programs. The opportunities for mismanagement are many. It is necessary to establish systems of accountability and to do this requires advanced monitoring and accounting practices, seldom available in developing countries.

Schools with book rental schemes must store the books between and during the school years, and care must be taken to ensure that books remain intact and clean. Many schools do not have the storage facilities or the security arrangements needed.

Any system has problems, and it is important to ensure that solutions are foreseen in the design of any book provision program. Despite complex management problems, the positive result of shifting costs to parents lies in higher efficiency in purchase, greater relevance of the materials, and savings in distribution due to the fact that books are reused and the students take better care of them. Any system of cost recovery must be supported by well-planned mechanisms for the provision of basic learning materials for students whose parents cannot afford to buy them. Experience in some countries has shown that it is possible to do this.

Distribution

The cost of distribution in publishing is a major one.[11] In commercial publishing, the cost of distribution is reflected in the sales price of a book. In contrast, the costs of distributing learning materials are rarely recovered by sales as most learning materials are distributed free of charge or sold at subsidized prices.

In the majority of developing countries, the need for a cost-effective distribution system for the delivery of the books is neglected. Most book development projects do not allocate funds for the building of a cost-effective and sustainable distribution system. In principle, the costs of distribution should be built into any book development project as a recurrent cost.

The cost of distribution is determined by policy. Decisions regarding the goals of book provision and the life of books must reflect physical realities and the costs required to establish the necessary infrastructure, to ensure the efficient distribution of learning materials. Many shortcomings in distribution systems are due to the lack of trained staff in the distribution chain and to uninformed policy decisions and unrealistic assumptions made by decision makers about the costs of distribution. Unplanned distribution will always be erratic and expensive.

The control of distribution costs is essential for an economic publishing program. The cost of distribution in urban areas where access is easy and the market relatively large, is estimated to be 25 to 30 percent of the total cost of a textbook. In inaccessible areas, the percentage is much higher—as high as 200 percent and more. According to the *African Book Sector Studies*,[12] it is quite possible that 50 to 60 percent of the overall cost of distribution could be spent in reaching 10 percent of the pupil population. The cost of reaching them may be unnecessarily high because no distribution network has been developed.

The costs of distribution are made up of expenditure on staff, premises, equipment and services. Wages and transportation costs have a tendency to exceed the budget. An annual budget for distribution must be provided to ensure delivery, whether distribution is handled by the government or subcontracted to private enterprise, or both. If the government meets the cost of distribution—either through subcontracting or through internal arrangements—it is important to remember that this cost is a subsidy.

The establishment of national warehousing is a capital asset, which needs regular maintenance and replacement. If funding is not provided on a regular basis, investments in all other areas will be ineffective because the books cannot then be delivered and stored.

Different unit costs apply to distribution: the cost per book, the cost per order, and the cost per consignment. Books with different distribution patterns—for example, textbooks and teachers' manuals—have different distribution costs. Those sold or distributed in single copies only have different costs from those distributed in sets.

A distribution policy must be formulated as a basis for planning the distribution operation. It must not be allowed to develop by accident or in isolation. The main elements in a distribution policy for the provision of learning materials are:
- goals for book provision (student/book ratios);
- expected lifetime of books and other materials;
- financing and cost recovery;
- sales or distribution structure (number and size of retail outlets to be served, order size);
- service level requirements;
- stocking; and
- the choice between subcontracting or government distribution.

While it is for educational planners to determine the goals of book provision and other policy matters, specialist knowledge is required to reach these goals.

Notes

[1] *World Bank Asia Region Book Investment Review.*

[2] Though importing books can be a good solution for some subjects, such as higher level education in science and technical subjects, there are a number of problems related to this practice. Imported instructional materials are often culturally inappropriate and a competitive price often results in poor quality. Furthermore, purchasing from outside required access to foreign exchange, which is not always available.

[3] According to *African Book Sector Studies: Summary Report* (Washington D.C.: World Bank, 1991), book scarcity has made book theft a major issue in most of the countries studied; the lack of adequate security in schools encourages theft.

[4] R. Harbison and E. Hanushek, *Educational Performance of the Poor: Lessons from Rural North-East Brazil* (New York: Oxford University Press, 1992).

[5] From *Instructional Media in Educational Planning and Administration and School Building: Teach Yourself Guide to the Management of Educational Media and Materials* (Paris: UNESCO, Educational Policies and Management Unit, n.d.).

[6] Malawi Special Distance Teacher Education Programme, Ministry of Education and Culture, *The Teacher's Handbook: Using the Local Environment* (Paris: UNESCO, 1993). (UNESCO doc. Ed-93/WS/28.)

[7] The Education for All program renewed discussion on the economic and social benefits of compulsory primary education. See C. Colclough with K.M. Lewin, *Educating All the Children, Strategies for Primary Schooling in the South* (Oxford: Clarendon Press, 1993) or, for a particularly interesting analysis, see Myron Weiner, *The Child and the State in India: Child Labor and Education Policy* (Princeton, N.J.: Princeton University Press, 1991).

[8] However, due to the general absence of long-term planning for book provision, any discussion about funding has a certain arbitrariness, as it remains almost impossible to plan beyond the present.

[9] P. Brickhill and C. Priestley, *Study on Textbook Provision in the SADC Countries* (Paris: UNESCO, 1993).

[10] Tony Read, *An Introduction to Textbook Projects* (n.d.).

[11] Book distribution has consistently been neglected in textbook projects; nevertheless, it is perhaps the single most important factor in improving existing systems for book provision. For an excellent training manual on the topic, refer to *Book Promotion, Sales and Distribution: A Management Training Course* (London/Paris: Book House Training Centre/UNESCO, 1991).

[12] *African Book Sector Studies: Summary Report* (Washington, D.C.: World Bank, 1991).

7

The Transition From State to Commercial Publishing Systems in African Countries

Paul Brickhill

This chapter offers insight into the problems and issues in the transition from state to private textbook supply underway in several African countries. The conclusions are based on studies I have done in Tanzania, Zambia, and Malawi, and observations and discussions with publishers from Mozambique, Ethiopia, Ghana, and Kenya. Zimbabwe, where my main experience lies, has a private system of textbook provision and provided a useful reference for transitions elsewhere. In revisiting documents, I find that my views have remained largely unchanged, albeit tempered by discussions with African publishers. I hope this chapter provokes as much as it informs.

Introduction

I would be a little suspicious of anyone described as an authority on the vexing question of the transition from state to commercial book provision. There are too many factors specific to one country, not least among them the economic and political terrain in which the process takes place. The real experts are the practitioners—publishers, booksellers, and educators—grappling with practical day-to-day problems. Nor am I convinced that rapid transition to a free market system alone offers the sole and unequivocal route to vibrant national book provision without regard for circumstances. In poor countries, poor people cannot afford books. Most African countries arrived at independence with little or no publishing infrastructure, compelling state intervention. Realistically, commercialization has to be accompanied by a national book policy to secure the "national character" of publishing, the needs of readers—for example, language policy—and all the components of the book chain, from authorship to distribution.

To pose the question, as one hears on occasion from enthusiastic advocates of private enterprise, only in terms of one system or the other is simplistic. If the transition is not understood as a long-term, ongoing process in the national interest to be supported until all components of the "book chain" function, failure is likely to be repeated. There is no quick fix. Book development demands long-term planning. Certain patterns are quite evident in this transition and common problems are emerging. It is these I wish to draw out and highlight.

The Background to State Intervention

State intervention in the book sector at the dawn of African independence was not as irrational as it appears today in the era of free market economics. A widely appealing concept in African nationalist political circles, it was seriously considered even in postindependent Zimbabwe as late as the mid-1980s, despite Zimbabwe's strong commercial publishing and bookselling base.

The main ingredient of state intervention was control over the textbook publishing industry, brought about by imposing a state monopoly to provide sufficient, appropriate, inexpensive (or free) textbooks for schools, invariably coupled with a new African-centered curriculum. Education was a highly charged political issue in postcolonial Africa. To most Africans, colonial education had been a "tool of the oppressor." Having been denied access to equal (or any) education in the past except in a few mission schools, many Africans felt they had been "educated" to perpetuate colonial rule and subjected to insidious anti-African attitudes in textbooks. On independence, nation building meant correcting the injustices of the past. The hunger for education was overwhelming in all of the new African states. Politically, education had to serve the needs of "the people," where the inherited system had been designed to exclude this. Expectations were fiercely high that education would "deliver" a new generation from poverty and oppression.

How was the textbook provision mechanism to function? There was overwhelming dependence on foreign authors and imported materials tied to the examination systems and curriculum of the former colonial power. Newly independent African countries had virtually no indigenous publishing capacity, outside of religious materials. Where subsidiaries of foreign publishers existed they exercised a monopoly over textbook provision, based largely on importing books from their parent company and sometimes reprinting these locally. The Lusophone and most Francophone countries had no publishing or printing infrastructure.

The State Provider Mentality

Against this background and the needs of rapidly expanding education systems and new curriculums, it was expected, and, indeed, responsible for the state to turn provider. The long-term prospects for an indigenous, commercial book sector were not apparent then. The economics of publishing, as an industry, was not understood because there was hardly a publishing industry. What was quickly required were large quantities of cheap or free textbooks—devised or adapted for local conditions—which only the state could provide. State intervention was not seen as merely an interim phase in a larger context of national book development.

The "state-provider" mentality became entrenched in the popular psyche in a few years and is now difficult to dislodge. As state textbook provision systems developed over the years, funded extensively by donors, the mentality strengthened, and the possibility of changing course grew more distant. The number of education ministry employees deriving their livelihood from state publishing grew, a bureaucracy of textbook provision grew, adherents grew, and the budget grew. The system justified itself. The budgets, unconstrained by profit and loss considerations and rationalized by the growing shortage of textbooks, grew steadily.

Arguments have been constructed over the years, in different settings, to justify continued state monopoly over textbook provision, even as it entered crisis. The alternative, where no indigenous publishing industry had emerged, seemed to be dependence on foreign books. Ironically, the fact that there was no indigenous commercial publishing or book trade capacity may have been itself an outcome of the state monopoly. Where local commercial publishers were established, the argument against business interests—"profiteering from the education of children"—has been put forward. This view can still faintly be heard in dusty corridors in many education ministries.

These arguments and those with a socialist ideological slant—central planning, and state ownership of the means of production, for instance—are secondary to the state-provider mentality. Whatever its initial intentions, it came to reinforce party control and the politics of patronage, which became in the broader context an overriding issue in African politics.

The Lack of Policy

The lethargy in developing mechanisms for book provision throughout Africa is effected by the lack of national data and policies related to culture in general, let alone book policies. African governments consistently refuse to pay serious attention to the chorus of independent media and cultural professionals saying that information is a strategic national industry and resource. As is the case in other strategic areas, it must be allowed to grow and function, secured by a sound conceptual framework, policy instruments, and, ideally, legislation.

African governments have not listened to their own publishing professionals. They have listened instead to their employees, and—where aid was concerned—to project consultants, few of whom will advise African governments to follow, or even investigate, international developments. Africa is typically regarded as unique and requiring different solutions.

How does Europe, for example, maintain its level and diversity of book output? Even a cursory examination reveals a history of indirect and direct support to national private publishing industries and of profound respect accorded to authors and a culture of literacy. The methods are innovative, diverse, and sophisticated, and include such things as buy-back systems, research and publishing subsidies, institutional support for writers and publishers—to strengthen the national language—and incentives to export. The weaker the industry—as in the case of smaller European countries with an insular national language—the greater the level of direct state support. The challenges to successful commercial publishing are not so different between continents.

Publishing is an activity that justifies support everywhere because it results in immense cultural, political, and economic advantages. Consider against this background the almost universal lack of political will throughout Africa even to keep a minimum public library system operating. Lack of funds? We all know about the debts and deficits of African governments, but the amounts required are small even in the tiny national budgets of African governments. Incentives that do not strain public funds are hardly considered. Books and publishing issues, especially in private hands, suffer from neglect and sometimes hostility.

If publishing can be likened to an "ideas factory," the true extent of damage inflicted by government neglect of books as a strategic industry in Africa can begin to be appreciated. An idea is born—technical, social, creative, or otherwise—and the publishing process transforms it into a definite and digestible form and disseminates it. There are, of course, other media channels, but none quite with the durability of the book. Books are read and reread, change hands, and require no technology to use. If flow of information is a direct and essential catalyst to social development, then government disincentives to publishing have stifled nation building in a far broader sense than "textbook provision." They have undermined the capacity to generate, shape, and share ideas. A generation of African thinkers and innovators have been in wasteland. Globally, Africa barely accounts for 1 percent of new book titles. What society can afford this?

Finally, in many African countries national interest has been subordinated to the politics of party and individual patronage too often. That this is not stated openly is central to our problem.

Some Effects of State Control

State subsidies and incentives to a strategic, commercial industry are clearly not the same as state control. One effect of state control in Africa has been to cripple nontextbook publishing. By taking the monopoly on textbooks—the profitable "rump" of publishing—the state has denied private publishers the possibility of subsidizing a general list with textbook sales. An equivalent scenario exists with booksellers. To remove booksellers from textbook provision in Africa is to eliminate them and with them their expertise and services.

Henry Chakava, as examples throughout the world confirm, has aptly observed that publishing is a "hands-on activity. It is a personalized trade that thrives best in the hands of individuals." Publishing and publishing industries depend on diversity of expertise. The relative health of any publishing industry can be accurately gauged by its level of diversity. For economic reasons, and particularly in Africa, this diversity can only develop in combination with access to the largest educational markets. Viability is the bottom line.

The importance of supplementary books and a significant number of authors are often mentioned in book studies. Supplementary books are generally published in situations where they can be combined with educational publishing. A truly competitive publishing industry, where state policy supports diversity and free markets, will encourage book diversity as well as a growing pool of specialized authors.

The publishing industry is inherently as broad and diverse as society. To succeed, it has to change as quickly as society. It is an accepted practice—in large publishers as well as small—that individuals take a publication from concept or manuscript to finished product. Publishing by committees, bureaucracies, and government departments is a caricature of real publishing.

Yet, despite the overwhelming evidence of the inability of state monopolies to sustain minimum book provision, there are success stories. Mozambique—one of Africa's poorest countries, wracked by civil war through the 1980s—produced more than 700 nontextbook titles from 1976 to 1989 in print runs ranging from 3,000 to 20,000. It is hard to see how this output could have been matched by a private sector, even if one had existed. Prior to the emergence of private publishers in the 1970s and 1980s, Ghana provided its primary school pupils with textbooks through state publishing, as did Zambia until economic pressures overwhelmed the country in the 1980s. With an economy based on state ownership, Tanzania had achieved an unprecedented degree of national literacy by the 1970s.

As much as publishing is a "hands-on" process, it also works within the parameters of economy of scale. Large economies of scale in publishing are more productive and cost efficient. This was the relative advantage of state publishing, particularly given the weakness, lack of financing, and inexperience in the private sector.

What therefore makes state publishing bad per se? First, there is a point in the development of economic infrastructure generally, and printing and publishing specifically, at which the capacity of the nation to provide books, independent of the state, exceeds the state's capacity. Where the state continues to cling to its monopoly, it retards publishing development. Book provision depends on the state's productivity, which—when properly managed—can have quite impressive results, but can never match the potential of the private sector. Second, monopolies in publishing rarely do more than provide basics and have a tendency toward wastage and inefficiency. The producer is not directly affected by the results in the way compelled by competition.

The Transition to Liberalization

The economic stagnation and crisis throughout Africa in the 1980s forced most African governments and their donors to reconsider their priorities. It is worth remembering that most state monopolies in publishing had become dependent on foreign aid by the 1980s. Governments did not have the money to sustain state textbook provision without it. Donors cannot excuse themselves entirely from the problems of state publishing, since in many cases they paid for it. It is not difficult to understand, despite some protestations to the contrary, that donors have had considerable influence over African book provision. As long as the money was available, few hard-pressed African governments were going to refuse it or the development approaches that went with it. The arrangement seemed to suit both government and donor.

In education development, since the 1970s and throughout the 1980s, the World Bank and other major bilateral donors worked as a matter of policy with governments. While some contact was established with private publishers and nongovernmental organizations (NGOs)—for instance, Scandinavian donors—typically these were confined to the "cultural desk" or the resident in-country mission. From the early 1990s the Bellagio Publishing Network has provided a forum for such contacts.

The World Bank had minimal contact with African publishers where education projects were designed in the 1980s, but on the whole the involvement of independent African publishing professionals has been absent from book provision projects. This left development professionals and government education planners to work out the mechanics of textbook provision systems, neither of which had much professional or commercial publishing experience. Thus, foreign consultants were used extensively to provide technical input, but many lacked a real or long-term grounding in African conditions. Mistakes were inevitable.

In November 1993, the African Publishers Network (APNET) dispatched its chairman, treasurer, executive secretary, and a well-known Tanzanian publisher to Washington, to introduce indigenous African publishing to World Bank officials and seek a reaction. It became clear from this mission and further contact that most World Bank officials, with one or two exceptions, were unaware of the extent, activities, and emergence of an indigenous commercial sector in African publishing—hardly news, by 1993, in African book circles. Moreover, it was apparent that some input, or lobbying, on key questions of African book provision was being provided, both directly and indirectly, by British and French multinational publishers.

It was entirely inappropriate that a major body of expertise in commercial publishing, indigenous publishers, hardly featured in the initial thinking about the privatization of African textbook provision. Yet, they held first-hand experience of commercial publishing in Africa, the nascent African book market, its perils, and its potential.

The first error in the privatization of African publishing was the failure to create what Chakava has referred to as a triangular partnership—donor, government, and African publishing professionals—as opposed to a vertical relationship. The need to approach privatization regionally—since African expertise tends to be concentrated in a few publishing centers—and the passive "wait and see" attitude of many African publishers, who were busy just attempting to remain solvent, forstalled this. This is a pity, as African publishers and booksellers not only had the day-to-day experience, they were in many cases further in their thinking than governments and donors about how commercial African textbook provision might work. It is crucial that these shortcomings are now being rectified, both as African publishing organizes itself regionally, through APNET, and by the Association for the Development of African Education (DAE) Working Group in Books and Library Materials—grouping donors to African education—that recognizes APNET as its African partner. Increasingly, but not yet consistently, African publishers are at least being consulted.

The move to break up state monopolies and liberalize was in the first instance the decision of donors, not governments. Elsewhere studies have traced the specific factors that stimulated the "new thinking" to the late 1980s. Clearly, the decisions applied by the major donors to African book provision were mirrored in most other sectors, reflecting the new wave of economic liberalism.

A key point was reached by the time of the 1991 Manchester conference on African textbook provision, where African publishers were minimally represented. After a decade of steadily increasing aid inflows to African education, donors seemed to have reached broad consensus that, at least in the long term, state monopoly textbook provision was futile. It had failed. The African education ministers and officials present were left with few illusions that change was imminent and necessary. Differences seemed to arise over the method of effecting the transition and whether a fast-track approach was preferable to gradual change.

The Breakdown in Control

Excessive state dependence on donor support had produced debilitating effects on textbook provision. Waste and inefficiency had become evident throughout state systems. A well-intentioned but nevertheless stifling bureaucracy maintained a monopoly over the publication and distribution of textbooks with donor support and had simply strained all the linkages in the "book chain" to breaking point. Governments embarking on the transition to commercial textbook provision have done so because donor-supported state mechanisms failed to ensure an adequate and sustained supply of textbooks to schools.

Of course, a host of factors came into play in each country, but the breakdown in control is a common theme. Corruption may be too strong a word, but the fact remains that productivity—defined loosely as the number of books reaching pupils' desks against total resources—was declining steadily as economic conditions deteriorated. It is fair to say that some individuals in the state system were corrupt in a petty sense, perhaps influenced by an unremittingly harsh economic background. The job stopped being done properly when families could not be fed. To compound matters, waste and inefficiency in the state system placed enormous burdens on the dwindling resources needed to keep the system going.

The critical weakness and main reason why control ultimately broke down as conditions deteriorated was that decisions, performance, and results did not directly affect the large number of people engaged in textbook production and supply. This lack of control or accountability in the state systems is well illustrated by the absence of reliable figures, and sometimes even estimates, of basic book data. Average pupil:book ratios, for example, varied wildly depending on the source.

Figures released in Tanzania in 1994 showed that over the previous five years, 94 percent of 17.4 million textbooks printed were delivered to district offices, but that the delivery from district storeroom to schools was uncertain. From statistics of books produced and sent to district levels, book:pupil ratios appeared to be in the region of 1:3 or 1:4.

A trial survey in 1994 on classroom usage of books in Tanzania concluded that book:pupil ratios were somewhat closer to 1:9 and there were extreme variations between schools and districts. A considerable number of books did not reach pupils. They either did not reach the school at all or were being held in school storerooms due to "uncertainty over future supply." An unknown proportion of books were already being purchased by parents, outside of the state system. In other words, parents were beginning to buy free state-produced textbooks from somewhere.

Less well documented is the extent of the industry's dependence on donor support. In the event of donor withdrawal, state systems in most instances would have collapsed. They were not sustainable without support. This triggered serious questioning of prospects for the long-term textbook supply.

Decision making has been a drawn out process, finally embarked on when a government was made to appreciate the extent of the crisis, acutely reflected in falling educational performance.

The Current Situation: Some Major Themes

While the transition to commercialization is in motion in Tanzania, Zambia, Mozambique, and Ethiopia, there appears to be lack of clarity in roles, time frames and operational details of future phases. Nobody knows exactly what their part will be in the machinery of textbook provision, including the consumer.

Without a definitive five-to-ten-year plan, the transition cannot be considered irreversible and yet it is clear donors will not support any reversal. The major element in textbook provision is planning. Any publishing operation relies on thorough planning because publishing itself is a process concerned with management of diverse resources—from authorship to financing, production, and distribution. One textbook may take two to three years just to develop, let alone a publishing program or distribution arrangement. The lack of definitive plans are perhaps understandable. The commercial system, itself underdeveloped and new to everybody involved, needs time to orient itself. Nevertheless, one senses confusion arising from the multiplicity of donors involved, advocating different priorities, subsidizing and stressing part but not all of the textbook system.

There is little apparent difference in overall objectives between donors. However, opinions vary considerably over some critical issues. Some donors tend to see indigenous publishing in a prominent role, while for others—including the World Bank—this is not a central issue. There are differences in approach to time frames. The Scandinavians seem committed to the phased and careful expansion of privatization while other donors prefer the fast-track approach. A prominent World Bank official called for the immediate privatization of textbooks in Tanzania on the grounds that it could not possibly be worse. He maintained that in a sample survey of households, 59 percent expressed discontent with availability of textbooks and that in his view parents could be relied on to pay for textbooks. He suggested that state assets in publishing be auctioned. The basic difference may be summed up as one approach that sees financing the market and freeing production quickly as imperative and another that sees the phased creation of capacity over a longer time frame as critical. The differences in donor approaches have contributed to the problem. In fact, the lack of clear decisions and leadership from these governments, especially in regard to a time frame for the transition, has contributed significantly to the confusion.

It is in the nature of books and education that many government departments and officials are involved in textbook provision. Only a few have professional publishing expertise and those that do have learned their trade under state monopoly. They also have different perspectives and interests in the outcome.

Moreover, the level of sycophancy in many African governments means that many decisions are referred to higher authority. Reaching decisions for this complex process requires careful preparation and has been a persistent problem. Among other effects, this has given external consultants tremendous influence. They enter this milieu as independent and impartial experts, able to prescribe solutions. In itself, this is not a bad thing, especially if it helps the process along. The problem is that it is a form of dependency. It does not develop the capacity of African governments to take informed and expert decisions in relationship to book provision. And it is expensive and impractical to rely completely on external technical input over a transition which will take perhaps eight years. Good technical knowledge is needed locally.

Governments have no experience in operating within a system of private-sector textbook provision. They are understandably cautious or even fearful. Officials and departments used to the state-monopoly approach in many cases hardly know where to begin, and many key decisions are needed rapidly. This is aptly seen in textbook approval systems, where a confusing array of possible approval systems present themselves. Which is the best? How fast can new systems be put into place?

In sum, it is obvious that governments—especially those under considerable pressure to effect the transition—are unclear about exactly how to proceed. Clear decisions for the medium term (five years) are needed quickly in order for publishers and everyone else involved to begin planning, preparing, and financing. They have not been made. Such decisiveness is hampered by the ministries implementing—rather than managing—the process and having to make too many decisions against a backdrop of inexperience in private-sector textbook provision.

The Indigenous Commercial Sector: The Driving Force

The most worrying element, however, is the apparent failure to recognize that the commercial sector must provide the impetus for change and demonstrate the technical proficiency required for textbook provision. The transition will occur successfully only to the extent and at the pace that the commercial sector can replace state textbook provision. An accelerated process is realistic only if the commercial sector is capable of meeting this challenge.

The tendency of ministries of education to retain decision-making authority, with the most important decisions having then to be cleared at a higher level, is worrying. It has the effect of slowing the empowerment of commercial publishing to which many publishing decisions must ultimately be devolved. Rather than being recognized as a full partner in the transition process with the education ministries and donors, the indigenous commercial sector is still a somewhat subdued element.

The problems posed by an infant industry—even one with highly experienced individuals—are real and cannot be underestimated, especially as regards financing and infrastructure. If indigenous commercial publishers and booksellers are unprepared for the challenge, the multinationals are not. In an accelerated liberalization, where emerging local publishers and booksellers face financing problems and shortcomings in technical expertise, foreign publishers stand to capture a considerable market share. Ultimately, it will be simply a matter of who is able to develop, publish, and place the manuscripts on the market more quickly. This places the indigenous commercial sector, once again, on the periphery with the exception of the privatized former state monopoly. It is unlikely that sufficient financial resources exist in the emerging local private sector to bear the risks involved with unrestricted competition.

Government's Role: To Implement or Manage

Ministries of education, concerned that an overly abrupt transition will seriously disrupt textbook provision, still perceive their function as one of implementing the transition, rather than "managing" it by delegating state-, private-, and NGO-sector resources to achieve the required results.

Serious flaws are found in this approach. The transition to commercialization is exceptionally difficult. Above all it requires that decision making has to be increasingly decentralized. The decision to publish any book, for instance, ideally must be at the risk of the publisher for the ethos of commercialization to mature. It should be a decision based on assumptions about the market, the product, the competition, financing, and returns. It cannot be effectively made in the "command" style of administration. The strategic problem here is that commercialization of the existing state monopoly does not automatically mean commercialization of the system, which requires competition. How does one break up the monopoly that provides the books and introduce the necessary "level playing field" in a situation where books are needed now and not in two or three years?

In Tanzania, the vehicle has been the Swedish International Development Authority-sponsored Pilot Project for Publishing (PPP), which has put selected textbooks out to tender to emerging commercial publishers. It has been an innovative approach. In Mozambique, the Instituto nacionale do livro is actively trying to promote small private publishers, while the former state textbook publisher, Editora Escolar, is being privatized. The role of private booksellers in school supplies has been recognized for some years and a commercial "book chain" is emerging. In Ghana, the state has launched a system of copublishing between state and private publishers. In Zambia the newly launched national book policy provides the beginnings of long-term policy.

The PPP in Tanzania, which is a commendable first stage, assumes a degree of centralization and control by the education officials and a gradual withdrawal by the state. It is precisely this withdrawal by the state that is problematic. The state retains a monopoly on all approved core manuscripts and works with specific textbook authors. Commercial publishers only enter the system through a strict but laborious tender procedure. The Ministry of Education retains absolute control of the market by making purchasing decisions centrally. Distribution remains centralized, effectively excluding the booksellers. In this mode of state control there is not enough room for the type of creative entrepreneurship demanded by publishing. Too much centralized planning in implementation exacerbates a bottleneck of decisions in an already overstrained system.

The capacity of the indigenous commercial sector will determine the outcome of privatization. Fundamental weaknesses include the failure to understand why empowerment of this sector is so urgent; why too much central decision making slows the process; and how the problems of an infant industry should be addressed.

Competition

If genuine competition is not achieved, the commercial system will suffer many of the shortcomings of the previous state monopoly. Growth, diversity of output, and a long-term commitment to issues such as national culture and language are not possible when one or two multinationals dominate the market.

Publishing in Zimbabwe provides ample evidence of success in this regard. To an overwhelming extent, creative writing, general books, children's books, national-language books, and for that matter book awards are the preserve of the small, struggling indigenous publishers, not the dominant textbook publishers, most of whom are subsidiaries or associates of Longmans and Macmillans.

Competition is only plausible when two conditions are met. First, when some emerging indigenous commercial publishers significantly reduce the financial and technical gap with their vastly bigger state and multinational competitors; and second, when approvals for multiple textbook are in place. It is difficult to comprehend the hesitancy of education officials on the second point. Surely a system where authors and their publishers have to compete openly results in better books and more innovation than a system where only a single author and book is allowed. Moreover, the latter is open to some level of malpractice. It centralizes a critical decision and relies entirely on the integrity and competence of everyone involved. It is not self-regulating.

The Purchasing System

The purchasing system will "drive" the new system under privatization. Assuming some form of per capita funding for textbook provision, the critical decision is precisely where and how the purchasing decisions take place. Centralized purchasing, still the case in Zambia, Tanzania, Ethiopia, and Ghana, reinforces the accumulated habits of the old system. Will schools have a choice of textbook for a subject, which implies competition? Or will purchasing simply mean schools will decide how many copies of the approved textbook they will buy? As a general principle, the further away the purchasing decision is from the actual user of the material, the less efficient the use of the funds.

Devolved purchasing on the other hand brings new problems, and transparency in this regard is essential. Decentralized purchasing can mean decentralized malpractice and problems of incompetence. There is an urgent need to train schools and education officers in the basic methods of purchasing, both on the administrative side and on textbook selection. The way these questions are approached will largely determine the future viability of local publishing and book provision.

Distribution

The number of volumes required for primary school core texts makes centralized supply viable, perhaps even desirable for a limited period. But as soon as one looks further, the distribution capacity of the book trade becomes critical. Upper secondary, tertiary, and professional schools require a greater number of titles and the market is spread more widely and in small pockets.

While it is possible to distribute primary and some secondary core texts through centralized channels, it is impossible with most other types of books. These require many points of sale and channels of access to reach their intended user. Without a healthy book trade infrastructure, potential buyers are without access. Lack of marketing and distribution, through bookshops, seriously inhibits all types of publishing, except large volume primary and secondary texts. This results in viability problems throughout the publishing system. Publishing needs backlists and diversity to strengthen their economic base. Backlists need consumers and many bookshops.

For various reasons, countries moving away from state monopoly publishing are still discouraging the development of a book trade.

Bookshops are still seen as unnecessary "middle-men," making books more expensive by taking a margin for themselves.

Centralized approaches to distribution appear attractive because through cutting out the retailer, creating a single distribution system, and concentrating supply lines, prices are lower. However, the cost to the book industry and book provision is great.

Bookshops, denied access to 85 percent or more of the market, become commercially untenable, cannot develop, and close down. As a result, overall access to books is greatly reduced; general and specialized publishers and lists are retarded; and quality declines with a lack of competition. This is how book industries lapse into a downward spiral of crisis management.

In the long term one must look toward significantly more effective distribution systems than those provided by state monopolies. One cannot promote commercial publishing unless people have access to books, and booksellers have access to the textbook market. It is unlikely that bookshops will develop quickly. It takes a considerable period to develop book trade skills. These are often learned on the job. Both donors and governments need to change their attitudes toward distribution and recognize the function of the bookseller in a commercial book industry. If there are no bookshops, the trade in general books collapses, readership suffers, book "awareness" and book "culture" are undermined, and all of this impacts educational development.

Economies of Scale, Intra-African Trade, and Regional Collaboration

If privatization is ultimately to achieve an independent, self-sustaining commercial book sector—rather than simply respond to crisis—it is impossible to avoid issues determined by economies of scale.

As an idea of what this means, two of Africa's more successful book industries, Kenya and Zimbabwe, represent a combined market of perhaps 5 percent of a small European country—such as Norway, Denmark, or the Netherlands—with an unique language and about one-ninth the population of the African nations. From a U.S. dollar per capita angle, Norway's book industry is about 150 times bigger than Zimbabwe's. This monetary comparison does not reflect volume or scope, since African books are about one-fifth the price of Norway's, but the comparison makes the point.

Publishers and book chain systems cannot function if the market they are working in is too small to support some economies of scale. This is particularly acute outside the primary and junior secondary textbook markets. Trapped in small domestic markets African publishers face an overwhelming constraint. In the long term, privatization must be accompanied by government efforts to promote intra-African trade in books, and regional collaboration. African publishers need access to bigger markets to fuel growth.

It is striking that regional approaches to book provision issues are so rarely mentioned. Solutions to certain problems can hardly be addressed unless a regional strategy is devised. Training and printing are examples. Publishing is such a broad activity that no African country will develop the full range of training required. Few countries in Africa will develop the scope of printing needed to service all publishing needs. Printing technology is developing rapidly and the costs of retooling with new technologies are beyond the means of many countries. Where solutions to pressing book problems are elusive at the national level, regional approaches should be explored.

Intra-African trade in books and printing presents considerable potential as a catalyst for improvement in book provision in many countries. In technical and scientific subjects, in some tertiary areas—for example, teacher training—and often in literature, the curricula or examination demands between several countries are so close as to be nearly identical. This is evidenced partly by the fact that multinational publishers have been able to slightly revise the same text all over Africa to comply with local curricula. Universities, teacher colleges, technical colleges, and other institutions throughout Africa are in many cases using an identical imported text.

The biggest obstacle to intra-African trade is ineffective information and marketing. To add to national bias, tariff barriers, lack of interest by development agencies, misunderstandings from governments, difficulties involved in starting, plus the practical problems of shipping, payments, and foreign currency have all served to inhibit intra-African book trade. It needs help.

The Goal: Getting the Book Chain Functioning

Privatization is merely one step, one of a series of measures aimed at creating a functioning, sustainable book chain. Book provision systems are, in reality, a complex set of linkages, a system of many components, evolved over a long period. This book chain is fragile even in the more robust African book industries. Policy priority must be to get the whole book chain system functioning at its most basic level with all of its components. This is the point from which book development starts in any meaningful way. Producing books and sending them out to schools is not book development until it takes place within a self-sustaining system of book provision. Because this fundamental issue is poorly understood by many civil servants and development professionals, whose background is not in books, lessons are not learned.

That books are the basic tool of education is undeniable, but that does not imply that educational experts are therefore the best people to manage book production and supply, or indeed that pedagogical considerations—for instance, curricula—provide the sole rationale in book supply. Book industries operate according to criteria determined by many factors outside the educational system. While educational considerations determine content and use, provision is essentially an industrial issue. Yet, this is precisely what educators forget when they enter into authorship, publishing, production, pricing, and supply and erect monopolistic barriers to exclude all others.

Much of the pain in the emergence of the book chain is still caused by short-term, inappropriate state and donor-influenced policy decisions. Curriculum developers and teachers are still writing books that should be written by a growing pool of semiprofessional writers and editing books that should be edited by publishers. Educational officials are still assuming the role of book distributor and bookseller, another technically demanding occupation, and attempting to manage book distribution systems. In their attempts to assume these roles, governments are distorting and retarding the normal emergence of the book chain.

Slowly emerging commercial book industries need financing, incentives, institutional support, and training. They need to operate in an environment relatively and increasingly free of state control, but in the "national interest." They need governments that understand how policy decisions effect the book industry, and how to coordinate these decisions with a long-term strategy to establish an indigenous book industry. Ad hoc decisions, hostility, and neglect will produce erratic performance and the need for constant and unsustainable donor support. While the macroeconomic environment has not helped, neither is it the principle reason why indigenous book industries in many African countries have failed to take root. A start has been made in the decision to privatize state monopolies, but it is only a start.

Unless dire circumstances dictate otherwise, governments should concentrate on achieving basic administrative goals to ensure optimum book use. These include storage, use, and conservation of books in the school system; development of libraries; basic administrative systems to purchase and deliver books to schools; adequate per capita financing of the book costs of the educational system; overseeing book content and quality control; and setting curricula, examinations, and standards. Otherwise the role of government is to ensure appropriate policy for the commercial viability of the book chain to provide the necessary books. This remains a goal, not a reality, but one that should be shared by all. It is a vital component of the book chain and the balance of responsibilities that promotes healthy book provision.

There is no fundamental conflict between the state and private publishing. Each has their role, their responsibility, and the need for close cooperation is essential. However, the economics of publishing industries have been misunderstood and there is a critical need for policymakers and donors to listen to publishing professionals.

This "book chain" view must be extended to professional book institutions and NGOs. Every publishing system needs them and they are in evidence in every successful book industry in the world. Their importance is underestimated in Africa. Indigenous NGOs involved in book development are often more effective than foreign NGOs because they are more responsive to local priorities and sensitive to a changing situation. They are also invariably more effective than governments because their objectives are better defined, and because they specialize in an area of development and are less bureaucratic.

More importantly, local NGOs act as agents of change, defining the needs clearly and introducing new approaches to old problems and changing conditions. They include professional associations and book councils, and their output will include the basic "tools" of book development—i.e., statistics and national bibliographies—that have not existed in much of Africa.

A brief, final note concerns the absolute necessity for a long-term national book policy. It is sometimes said that many successful book industries do not have a "book policy." This is simply not true. It may not be written down in so many words in a document, but policy formulation exists. The main considerations in a national book policy are not its content as such, which must change with circumstance, but that all the players—all government departments concerned, the development sector, and the private sector—are involved in and committed to its design; that it is conceived as a continuous, evolving, and flexible process to be modified and improved; and lastly, that it must be implemented, mistakes and all, with government support.

The effect of book policies in countries such as India, Colombia, and Greece—all somewhat closer to African reality than Western Europe—deserve study to appreciate how significantly book policy—and in some cases legislation—can improve book provision.

8

Electronic Publishing: New Technologies and Publishing

Czeslaw Jan Grycz

Since the advent of computers—and especially of personal computers—the vocabulary of the publishing industry has been enriched by an influx of unfamiliar acronyms and phrases. Many of these sound intuitively easy to understand, but may have specific counterintuitive or ambiguous meanings. *Electronic publishing* is just such a term. It sounds easy to understand. Yet, if one were to ask a representative handful of publishers to define its meaning, there would very likely be several quite divergent definitions.

Using jargon and technological terms in a chapter on electronic publishing is unavoidable. However, concepts discussed here will be expressed in ways that are intended to be straightforward and understandable. After reading through this review, readers may remain unable to define electronic publishing. They will—it is hoped—be more aware of why there exist so many diverse definitions.

Computers and Publishing

It is self-evident that computer science developed in isolation from its potential interaction with publishing. In the 1970s—save for the extent to which computer scientists sought to publish research in academic and research journals—contact between computers and the publishing industry was virtually nonexistent. Yet in that short space of time, the computer and publishing industries have become inexorably bound together in the marketplace created by desktop publishing, distributed networked information, and the entrepreneurial subcultures that these have spawned. Had there been deliberate and conscious interaction in the formative decades of the 1960s and 1970s, one can speculate that a number of problems might have been resolved differently: Publishers might have entered their "electronic age" earlier and a more useful selection of authoring and editing tools might have been developed.

FROM TEXT EDITORS TO WORD PROCESSORS

Computer scientists appear to have faced—early on—several important obstacles. Not the least of these was that as computing capabilities increased in sophistication so did the sheer number of algorithmic instructions (lines of program code) required to instruct a computer to accomplish a given task. And as programs became longer and more complex, engineers faced increasing management difficulties in locating and correcting errors in the code. Debugging programs—that is, locating the source of an error and correcting it—is tedious. (Incidentally, it is a tedium familiar to editors involved with similar tasks—converting manuscripts into publications.)

Programmers naturally turned to computer-assisted methods to solve their difficulties. They developed computerized tools that facilitated their ability to correct errors in code. Utilizing the capacity of video monitors to display alphabetic characters, programmers represented code instructions as statements on a screen. Next, they developed handy applications with which they could identify individual lines of program code; enter editorial modifications on them; and finally, reinsert the corrected lines in their proper sequence within a program, in place of the defective ones. The generic name for such applications was *text editors*. As they were primitive precursors of *word processing software*, it is instructive to consider component elements of these programs.

By design, text editors emphasized *content* over appearance. The *form* of displayed lines was relatively unimportant. It is easy to speculate, however, that not long after text editors became widely available in computer labs, engineers wanted to print their program codes onto paper in order to more comfortably proofread or store the code. Others might have been involved in preparing scientific papers for publication. Using the handy and available text editors to write narrative text instead of programming code was convenient. A natural consequence of composing narrative text (the verb "composing" reveals it) was a desire to arrange the words in a more attractive way than was possible on a simple programmer's line printer. Hence, the gradual addition of functions that permitted, at first simple, then increasingly complex layout and positioning of text on paper. At first, formatting was made possible through a series of "add-on" modules designed to solve one problem at a time, and without any overall contextual consideration. Ultimately, these programs evolved into specialized applications in their own right.

Because developers of text editors initially possessed only modest opinions about why format might be important, their engineering solutions were suitably simple. Later, the lack of overall context or standards would wreak havoc both on the computer and publishing industries. Compatibility within systems was frustrated by a lack of unified theory. Interoperability across platforms was hampered. Integration of equipment into existing businesses was thwarted. Broad-based business opportunities were spoiled.

CONTENT VERSUS FORM

In text editing programs, *content* was distinct from *format*, and each was treated independently. In modern programs the demarcation is not nearly as clear, which leads to operational ambiguities within the workplace, too. A persistent present-day quandary for managers of publishing enterprises is how to define the proper role of an editor. Historically, editors were concerned exclusively with content issues. Increasingly, however, they are able to involve themselves in domains that were once the exclusive prerogatives of the designer (who was previously restricted to aesthetic tasks concerning format). Today, the distinctions are increasingly arbitrary, since even modest word processing programs permit the simultaneous manipulation of both content and form. Would-be editors and would-be designers need to know considerably more about the role played by their opposites, as well as mastering computing techniques that will be employed in the pursuit of their jobs.

STYLE OR STRUCTURE?

There exist quite different philosophical approaches to handling format. One approach favored integrated word processing and powerful page layout programs. In their turn, these fostered the creation of page description languages. Paul Brainerd, of the Aldus Corporation, coined the phrase *desktop publishing* to describe the advanced layout capabilities made possible *on the desktop*, as a result of harnessing page-description languages, font outline specifications, and layout programs (such as Brainerd's own popular PageMaker). PostScript is currently the leading page description language of choice for this group. Computer programs evolving from this philosophy are characteristically *interactive*, with powerful capabilities. Users of such programs must, however, be willing to manipulate text and images on screen in real time in order to create ultimately acceptable pages that can be stored or printed.

Because PostScript has become so popular, a very wide range of computer application programs currently supports PostScript. A common subtheme of technological advance involves "leapfrogging," in which one program overtakes another in terms of capabilities. This evolutionary character may be merely a marketing opportunity for software developers, but for traditional publishers—familiar with conventional decision making about capital investments—the proliferation of options for software, alone, is decidedly frustrating.

Based on the PostScript standard, advances have also been made that enable PostScript files to directly generate film-imposed flats, printing plates, and even to control ink-jet printers. Such capabilities point to the emergence of a viable "on demand" publishing capability. This is surely a major component of electronic publishing. In the college textbook market, traditional publishers—like McGraw-Hill—have already launched operations designed to capitalize on such capabilities. In a project called PRIMIS, McGraw-Hill (in association with the University of Southern California and the University of California, San Diego, and other institutions of higher education) is experimenting with customized textbook manufacturing. Interestingly, the college bookstore has been identified as a likely partner in such an enterprise. The cost of PostScript-compatible printing technology is sufficiently low to be able to place it at the optimal delivery point: within the college bookstore itself. But the emphasis of interactive page makeup has its detractors, too.

An opposing approach to formatting emphasizes the development of standards for describing document *structure*. Advocates of this approach point to the fact that if a structure is properly identified, it is possible to create a simple *style sheet* by which various structural elements of a manuscript are to be displayed. Style sheets, in this context, are not much different from electronic typographer's instructions. Structural tags, advocates claim, give ultimate flexibility in formatting. Structural tags can be interpreted, for example, by one style sheet that formats the text for use in a two-column academic journal. The same document can be displayed as a three-column article (an alternative format) simply by changing the definitions in the style sheet. Furthermore, structural tags are more compact than are page descriptions, so text can be stored more efficiently. Finally, structural tags may facilitate access to the text. Some searching programs can rapidly access subhead levels and other structure elements to efficiently reach a desired location within lengthy text streams.

Structural document definition is, perhaps, best expressed through *standard generalized markup language* (SGML)—the development of which is a high priority for advocates of this approach. SGML has become very popular within the optical storage community, concerned as it is with storage and access problems associated with large amounts of information. Structural knowledge can be very effectively used by programmers of complicated searching algorithms for finding desired information quickly. Academic and research institutions, too, for whom archiving is critical, see SGML as a means of protecting against rapid technological obsolescence. Whereas page description is a relatively proprietary area of software development, SGML tags are expressed in standard ASCII (American Standard Code for Information Interchange) and are thought to be immune from proprietary software changes. It must be admitted, however, that proponents of SGML face considerable obstacles.

Page description languages are supported by software that is decidedly "user friendly," whereas programs that facilitate identifying document structure are considerably less so. Furthermore, for many individuals, the concept that documents possess structure has proven difficult to understand.

Several companies have recently rededicated themselves to the development of easy-to-use SGML software. Since the U.S. federal government adopted a Computer-Aided Logistics Support [CALS] initiative, a wide, new potential market for such programs has been created. CALS is an implementation of SGML, mandated to be used by government contractors in submitting bids and proposals. The government has been convinced that structural tagging will permit improved management over the array of proposals and documents it receives from its contractors. Similarly, SGML is popular within the military for its documentation needs, since large volumes of information must be handled efficiently. European publishers, it should be noted, have taken a lead over American publishers in adopting to SGML conventions. How this will relate to the future competitive advantage of American publishers remains to be seen.

PRINTER TECHNOLOGY

Meanwhile, other specialists anticipated eventual problems with output and print technology and began, simultaneously, to address challenging complications related to various imaging capabilities. Many of the most popular typesetting machines of this era (1970–1980) depended on photographic master negatives made from classic letterpress typefaces. The bizarre mechanics that resulted from efforts at mechanizing the process of setting type is a history of creative ingenuity peppered with a record of commercial failures. The sheer variety is hard to exaggerate. John W. Seybold documents these in considerable detail in his comprehensive book, *The World of Digital Typesetting*.[1]

Clearly, what the personal computer industry needed was an entirely new print technology, and it finally came in the form of a PostScript-compatible laser printer, not unlike those used for office copiers. Ultimately, a full range of output devices from inexpensive to professional and from line printer-quality to high-end-typographic-quality were developed. Each had licensed PostScript interpreters, and could accept files from a variety of personal computer applications programs. Such capabilities in the general consumer marketplace were to change the face of publishing. At the time of their appearance, most publishers were ignorant of their ultimate impact.

A wag once proclaimed that "Freedom of the Press belongs to those who own one." The truth of that statement was demonstrated in the 1980s and 1990s, when all manner of entrepreneurial publishers produced a high volume of very interesting titles, indistinguishable from titles produced by established publishers and largely produced on inexpensive equipment. Entrepreneurial publishers, were, in fact, now able to "own" (electronic) printing presses: personal computers and PostScript output devices. With such modest equipment, even small publishers could produce professional-looking publications. If the individuals starting such entrepreneurial businesses also possessed the intellectual, editorial, aesthetic, and marketing skills necessary to conduct a publishing business, they were, indeed, publishers. Because both their capital investment and their plant costs were lower than those of traditional publishers, they could enter the marketplace with competitively priced books.

Previously, traditional publishers controlled the outlets or "gateways" by which authors reached their audiences. Desktop publishing opened up many more gateways. A large variety of publications flooded the market: some good, and some inferior. For many, the established gateways had been viewed as barriers to publication. Now that the barriers were all but eliminated, the public began to realize the value of the gatekeeping functions themselves and the importance of the imprints conferred upon certain works by established publishers. A publisher's traditional peer review and copyediting functions, it turned out, also guaranteed a certain quality standard. Such standards were not universally guaranteed in the entrepreneurial environment of desktop publishing.

Trends in the Typesetting Industry

Now it is time to review a quite different industry, one that emerged centuries ago directly from the printing and publishing guilds of the Renaissance: typesetting. Typesetters were originally masters of hot metal matrices or reusable metal (often lead) characters. Such characters were *composed* into pages on instruction from the publisher. Pages were prepared for print when they were *imposed* into position for specific printing presses. The typesetting industry has changed little through the centuries, even up to the present. Typesetters were, however, among the first to feel the impact of computerization when computers penetrated their markets, because the typesetting business was almost equally capital- and labor-intensive.

Typesetters held substantial investments in hot metal font magazines. Many successful typesetters also had significant portions of their inventory locked up in forms. There was, after all, a strong inclination to keep typeset pages that might be expected to reprint in a foreseeable future. It was not sensible to redistribute the type into cases for certain jobs (because that would not only necessitate retypesetting in case of a reprint, but also the ancillary and no less expensive proofreading and correcting functions). Labor was highly skilled and costly. In order to create aesthetic pages from the relatively nonmalleable metal slugs, master craftsmen developed unique and specialized talents. Functions such as kerning and letterspacing took time. Mastery of the appropriate uses of special ligature and sort characters involved a long apprenticeship and commitment. Even keyboarding required considerable experience, since it involved operating complicated keyboards and equally complicated typesetting machines.

Typesetting machinery could only be as productive as an individual keyboarder could be fast and accurate. When Merganthaler introduced its variable input phototypesetter (VIP), it sought to maximize equipment utilization by making it possible for a single piece of hardware to handle input from a variety of sources. Merganthaler had long enjoyed a commanding presence in the typesetting equipment industry. When the company modernized its line of equipment, it became possible to produce type not only from direct keyboarding, but also from sources as diverse as paper tape, magnetic diskettes, or telecommunication transmission. What was intended as a beneficial economic efficiency drove a wedge between the function of the keyboarder and traditional typesetting skills. Such separation had already been anticipated by Ludlow and Monotype, each of whom produced machines that could be driven by punched paper tape as well as direct keyboarding. But it was not until the introduction of the Merganthaler VIP machine, in an economic environment already pressured by competition from personal computers and desktop publishing software, that typesetters realized they could easily employ cottage and even inexpensive offshore keyboarding labor (especially for complex mathematics and scientific equations) to more efficiently utilize their expensive batch-driven typesetting equipment and inventory of hot metal fonts.

Once the wedge had been driven home, typesetters began to think of their businesses as comprising separate cost centers for input and output functions. A lively competition emerged among what became known as *front-end* software designers. Companies such as PENTA, BEST, and CompuGraphics developed very sophisticated typesetting drivers for a variety of specialized typesetting applications. The function of the front-end program was to establish the guiding principles by which pages could be appropriately typeset. The front-end program acted as a kind of filter through which the text stream could be passed. The rules, established by the front-end software, would cause the text stream to be assembled into attractive pages. Still a classic, Stan Rice's *Design Aspects* and its companion, *Systematic Design,* instructed type designers to think in structural and modular terms so that their marked-up manuscripts would run smoothly through a batch-driven front-end system.[2]

As competition for typesetting business increased, more comprehensive front-end programs were purchased, and these inevitably replaced skilled craftspersons. As expensive skilled employees retired, they were frequently replaced by less-skilled keyboarders, based on the belief that typesetting layout skills had migrated to the computer-programmed front-end software.

While some companies bucked this trend, the skills within the typesetting industry as a whole declined and gradually disappeared. In their decline, typesetters inevitably pushed back upon publishers responsibilities whose fulfillment was once the pride of the typesetting industry. Many typesetters began to consider themselves service bureaus. Many publishers hired proofreaders and page-makeup artists in an effort to compensate for the (now largely absent) skills that were once a part of the services provided by typesetting vendors. Not incidentally, typesetters could ill afford to keep skilled labor anyway, because they were simultaneously being pressed to reduce their costs by publishers facing competition from the personal computer and desktop publishing entrepreneurs. This circular effect made it economically impossible for many typesetting vendors to avoid the very cost-cutting measures that publishers chided them for taking.

In order to counter downward economic forecasts, typesetters cast about for ways of leveraging their investment in equipment. Several typesetters established business partnerships with color separation firms, and vice versa. Currently, most typesetters provide some form of front-end color separation services. Similarly, many traditional color separators provide typesetting as an adjunct to their separations and layout work. The common strategy is to provide full service and high quality. In both cases, the high quality can only be had from sophisticated and expensive equipment. The amortization of equipment expense across a wider range of potential clients makes such partnerships attractive.

Traditional publishers adapted easily to changed vendor relationships, even if they resisted their own computerization. By the time of these marketplace adjustments, however, publishers *had* experimented with a wide variety of computerized front-office applications, and had developed a certain internal competence with computer programs. There existed relatively inexpensive preview applications that permitted traditional publishers to begin experimenting with page and color layouts without taking the risk of handling live jobs. The professional output could still be generated by vendors on the high-cost, sophisticated equipment in which they invested. The publishers could, once again, avoid having to make capital investments of the type that would draw them into managing departments not within their essential business mandate: the selecting and making public of books. This compromise (practiced even now) provided economic and business advantages for both parties. It reduced costs, nearly eliminating alterations costs for the publisher, and provided for more efficient and more productive operations for the vendor.

The distinguishing characteristic of the typesetting and prepress industries was an emphasis on *batch processing*. In order to amortize capital equipment costs, equipment needed to be utilized to its maximum capacity. This could not be accomplished through interactive processing, it was thought, but only through batch processing, in which text was "poured" through a front end, and the machine merely processed one job after another.

Typesetters, observing the growing infatuation with desktop publishing, wondered whether desktop publishing would diminish their market. Most concluded it would not—believing, instead, that the desktop publishing phenomenon would take over a variety of publications that might previously have been too expensive to typeset: newsletters, promotional flyers, and point-of-purchase displays. This effect, they argued, would raise typographic standards for that market segment. In turn, this would increase the market for typesetting itself, bringing new customers from among the lower segments of the market.

Typesetters were both wrong and right. Desktop publishing grew more rapidly than anyone expected, and with it came a growth in program sophistication that first challenged and later matched that provided by many of the front-end batch programs. Appreciation for typeset quality also rose. Ironically, there is more written today about typographic excellence than there was in its supposed hot metal heyday. Business for typesetters has remained somewhat stable, but only because many typesetters have, themselves, adopted desktop publishing techniques with which they can—because of their long experience—produce high-quality and elegant type under traditional arrangements with publishers. Publishers have not, as a rule, concerned themselves with the equipment used by a vendor to generate type—so long as the quality, price, and delivery are reasonable.

Ironically, publishers were insulated from the impact of computers on the typesetting and prepress industry by the very capacity of those businesses to realign themselves to changing market conditions, to form new partnerships, and to absorb new technologies able to keep them competitive and priced at levels that did not trigger changes in relationships with publishing clients. Some publishers, for their part, experimented with what they thought would be a low-cost alternative to typesetting services by purchasing desktop publishing equipment and setting up desktop publishing departments. Many discovered that internal administrative costs were more than the expected cost advantages. Most decided that it was not in their best interests to become involved in this form of electronic publishing.

The paradox is that the differing economic forecasts were correct, even though many decisions turned out to be wrong. Typesetters wanting to adopt new desktop publishing technologies, believed they would have to retool from a batch mode of operation to an interactive one, and felt it was largely unwise to do so. Publishers, desiring to bring back in-house what they no longer could satisfactorily obtain from vendors, predicted they would have to reeducate staff to perform new functions, and would have to accept potentially expensive new management responsibilities. Desktop publishing developers felt they could not quickly satisfy the quality standards demanded by traditional publishers who were used to professional typesetting output.

Neither typesetters nor publishers justified the integration of desktop publishing into their operations on the basis of economic advantage. It is still not at all clear whether shifts to desktop publishing are economically productive. The perception is widespread, however, that a publisher that operates an internal typesetting facility (whether traditional or desktop-oriented) achieves a considerable improvement over the degree of control it has over its work. This is seen to be competitively advantageous and, probably only after that, economically valuable. Publishers who operate sophisticated desktop publishing departments frequently claim to be involved with "electronic publishing."

Different conditions in each environment caused a shift in balance that permitted a move toward electronic solutions. For typesetters it was economic viability, coupled with a brief spate of the distasteful mechanical problems that plagued phototypesetting equipment during the short transitional period between hot metal and digital type, and that permitted disenchanted typesetters to look elsewhere for solutions. During the period in question, typesetting devices were photomechanical. They relied on computer-driven elaborate mechanical carousels of disks of photographic negatives. The machine needed to locate a desired character on a spinning disk and flash a strobe light through the negative on the disk. It also needed to expose a piece of photosensitive paper while the disk was in position, and properly focused at the appropriate type size. This proved troublesome to accomplish.

For publishers, there was an appreciation for the front-office work that personal computers provided. Word processing and accounting spreadsheets had become ubiquitous, even if manuscript processing had changed but little. Gradually, designers were using computer programs to generate book or jacket designs. Editors were continually reporting complaints from authors who were convinced that the manuscript they had prepared on their computers could be used to provide typeset material less expensively than the process proposed by the editor. For authors, the choice was simple. In a package about the size of a typewriter, and only slightly more expensive than executive models of typewriters, they could purchase facilities for word processing, footnoting, editing, cross-referencing, and creative work, and still have applications that could be used by various members of the household for other purposes.

The Development of a Consumer Marketplace for Electronics

The event that catalyzed development and change was a simple and unexpected one: the widespread enthusiasm for computerized word processors by a class of users who might be called "authors." Desktop publishing capabilities were attractive to authors because—it turned out—authors cared deeply about the ultimate appearance of their publications. In the print environment, capital investments incurred by publishers (and by extension, by typesetters in the labor of composing pages), were so great that they determined contract terms that protected such investments. In order to do so, virtually all control over publication resided with the publisher.

The introduction of low-cost computers equipped with software applications that produced acceptable typesetting quality changed contract negotiations. Authors soon invested their own capital, and maximized their investment by adding to it the labor of mastering skills, and interactively producing typeset pages of considerable quality and professionalism. It did not take long for authors to demand a return on their investment through contract negotiations with publishers.

Prior to the introduction of new technologies, the process of publication was essentially linear. Describing publishing activities was relatively easy and straightforward. While there were differences in organizational structure from one publisher to another, they were principally differences of emphasis.

The overall process of publishing could generally be described as including the following discrete stages:
- acquisitions

- editing
- design
- typesetting
- proofreading
- layout
- page makeup
- printing
- binding
- warehousing
- fulfillment

During the 1970s and 1980s, however, after the widespread introduction of personal computers within publishing firms, the comfortable linear processing deteriorated. It not only dissolved within publishing enterprises, but also in the relationship between author and publisher. The relative advantage of learning and mastering even complicated software favored individual investment of time. Conversely, corporations and large organizations still faced a plethora of compatibility problems, coupled with larger gross investment for equipment acquisition and maintenance. This meant that authors (who traditionally were at a disadvantage when negotiating with publishers) began to assert their stronger negotiating position. They not only perceived they were bringing improved quality to the negotiations (electronic diskettes, sometimes in camera-ready-copy format), but they also appeared to bring greater knowledge to the table (since publishers, facing greater barriers, had not developed uniform experience with electronic capabilities and computer technologies).

Transforming a manuscript into a publication, while still involving the same functions, is no longer linear, but modular. What once were very distinct and specialized functions began to be performed by individuals without traditional specialized training. The boundaries between departments have eroded, as have boundaries between independent business entities within the publication stream. Handling manuscripts electronically forced editors to be more cognizant of design decisions. Designers began, in some houses, to make editorial decisions. Editors began to make typesetting decisions. Publishers who historically depended on external vendors found it possible to consider various options and perform numerous tasks within their own offices prior to spending out-of-pocket money for vendor services. Authors began to wonder whether they themselves might enter the publishing field and engage in self-publishing, as a number of their colleagues were doing.

MANAGEMENT

Clearly, all these changes have significant managerial and economic implications for publishers. Today, decisions about which functions to keep in-house, and which to job to outside vendors can be quite different. Partnerships have evolved between publisher and supplier on the basis of technological integration. Authors' status has changed, too, and many publishers are now rethinking the appropriate terms of author contracts. In the vanguard that academic and scholarly environments sometimes are, there have been serious suggestions that authors retain their copyright. Traditionally, these have been contracted to publishers, but some feel it is advisable for authors to reconsider this long-accepted policy.[3]

Publishers have historically been inclined to keep a very low essential overhead, and to "outsource" as much of their variable costs as possible. This has permitted them a certain insulation from the personnel difficulty of production cycles (exacerbated by seasonal bookselling cycles). It has also permitted access to a flexible and varied workforce, such as might be needed for the production of quite different types of publications. The skills needed to produce a first-rate cookbook, for example, while related, are different from those needed for a biology textbook.

ECONOMICS

The economics of publishing depends on two activities: *selecting* appropriate materials to bring to the attention of the public, and sales through *publication* (making public). By reducing the costs of manuscript acquisition, vetting, and manufacturing (selecting functions that are typically described as *plant costs* in economic terms), publishers reduce costs and are therefore able to market their books and journals for a lower price (or a higher margin of profit). By reducing the cost of duplicating, disseminating, and delivering copies of their publications (publication functions that are typically described as *edition costs* in economic terms), publishers similarly reduce costs. But the latter can bring additional benefits: improving timeliness of service or adding values to a publication—values that differ from those provided by print.

Economic models consistent with physical, printed artifacts are well known. Investment is made in selecting and publishing. Profits or surpluses are generated by selling the finished products to purchasers at cost plus margin of profit. The publisher has some flexibility in pricing strategies that depend on judgments and risks taken in establishing print runs. The higher the print run, the lower the unit cost and (presumably) the price. But printing a large number of copies increases the investment, as well as the risk that a proportion of the print run will remain unsold, or will have to be inventoried for a long time. The converse is also true: if a publisher chooses a lower print run, the investment risk is reduced; but each copy of the print run will cost more (there will be a higher *unit cost*). This will necessitate a higher sales price. There is a point at which potential buyers will be dissuaded from making a purchase (*price resistance*) because they may judge that the cost is greater than the perceived value of the publication.

Publishers have jockeyed these factors in various ways. Many publishers initially release hardcover editions (which have historically commanded premium prices). Later, they release softcover editions (which are perceived to require aggressive pricing strategies). By distributing plant and edition costs in such a way as to maximize potential margins in each market, publishers have been able to subsidize certain editions at the cost of others. Subsidiary rights sales for serialization, translation, or book club markets are time-proven methods for maximizing investment and improving margins. No matter how the variants are played, the essentials do not change.

COPYRIGHT

Economic realities must be understood in order to comprehend publisher contract conventions, and the overarching copyright law. Since marketing identical titles could result in an unruly marketplace, publishers have demanded that authors yield *exclusive rights* to represent and publish their works. Since the availability of additional copies (or copies produced at a lower cost) would tend unfairly to undermine the value of an original publisher's investment, the copyright law protects the publisher's investment and competitive position by prohibiting copying. The law even provides for *fair use*, a concept that establishes the amount or frequency of lawful copying by end users, recognizing that some copying ought to be permitted.

A library, for example, is prohibited from purchasing a single copy of an expensive publication and copying an unlimited number of photocopies for its patrons. Fair use and copying are nettlesome issues for print publishers because the enforcement of such provisions is difficult. Wide dispersal of printed copies makes it very difficult to establish means for enforcing compliance with the copyright law. Nevertheless, mechanisms (largely based on an honor system, reinforced by selective litigation) have been put in place that sufficiently reassure print publishers that their rights are protected. It ought to be added that the copyright law functions to reassure and encourage authors, too. The preamble to the copyright law states as its main purpose the encouragement of creativity by authors, not the protection of economic interests for publishers.

Publishers have no such level of comfort with electronic publishing. The conditions of publication are considerably different, the conventions are not well established, and the copyright law was not written in anticipation of electronic publishing. Some people claim that the copyright law is sufficiently flexible to embrace electronic publishing, while others are not so certain.

Optical Storage

The medium of print publications is largely paper. What is stored on the paper are images of alphabetic characters. But alphabets (as well as other nonalphabetic characters) can be represented by digital analogs to typeset or calligraphed images. Digital images can be stored on media other than paper: including electronic, magnetic, or optical media. Some publishers calling themselves electronic publishers might, at one extreme, merely reproduce existing print publications on magnetic or optical media. In fact, it would not be wrong to suggest that most traditional publishers enter the electronic publishing market in just this way. Fewer publishers are publishing original material in electronic form. Curiously, those that are involved in the new forms often have less experience and fewer credentials in traditional print form, yet they are more properly electronic publishers in the true sense. Publishers who utilize electronic media in place of paper (i.e., journals on diskette, or publications on CD-ROM disks) see advantages in them as a means for disseminating large amounts of information in convenient packages. The (electronic, magnetic, or optical) media are used exclusively as vehicles for dissemination.

One would be tempted to believe that such an adaptation of media to the traditional publishing process is insignificant. It would seem that the essential characteristics of ownership do not change; nor that fundamental publishing economics would be modified. The behavior of publishers suggests otherwise. Perhaps because of the quantity of information that can be provided on a CD-ROM disk, and surely because of the relative ease with which information can be copied from such disks, publishers have quickly adopted quite different conventions for protecting their rights than pertain in print. The most conspicuous difference is publishers' reliance on contract law to establish the relationship between publisher and user. To the extent they do so, publishers undermine the possibility that the copyright law can expand to afford protection in an electronic environment. Ironically, many publishers assert that copyright expansion is a goal as they increasingly rely on contract law instead.

Most publishers of information delivered on CD-ROMs require the signing of a license agreement, which spells out the terms and conditions of ownership and use. The terms of a license agreement constitute a contractual relationship between publisher and buyer. The terms of such a contract can differ considerably from what the buyer may expect. For example, libraries subscribing to printed periodical publications are accustomed to conventions by which they clearly own the copies that are paid for and delivered to them. If a subscription to a periodical publication is canceled, the library expects to receive no additional copies beyond what it had paid for. Neither does it expect to be required to return those copies that have already been delivered. Under the terms of some *license agreements*, however, these counterintuitive terms are often the prevailing ones.

In fact, the "subscription" to a licensed CD-ROM disk may well permit a library to use and access the disk, receive regular upgrades, and be sent regular issues in a deceptively standard manner. But should the library decide to cancel its subscription, it might be surprised to find that the terms of the license agreement require it to return all the disks it received (even past issues) to the publisher. The library will perceive itself to have *rented* access to the information contained on the disk for only the length of time it was paying "rent." And it would be right in perceiving matters in this way. Such differences have led publishers to consider entirely new economic models for electronic publishing. These include the following:

1. *Site licenses.* Publishers establish a price, covering existing costs for "first copy" editing, peer review, and data preparation for a "large area site license." The licensee redistributes data to its subscribers using any media deemed appropriate.
2. *Acquisition on demand.* Articles are deposited in file servers, unbundled from physical journals or books. Quality signifiers

(e.g., publishers' imprint, peer review recommendations, number of retrievals) replace the present positional relationships (some journals are more respected than others). Price could vary, depending on such criteria as the "importance" of the document, timeliness of access, and the status of the document retrieved (e.g., preprint, accepted-for-publication, reviewed, published).
3. *Discipline-specific literature base.* Articles are deposited in file servers, according to discipline, for access by specific research communities. The database includes current work, work-in-progress, previously published texts, and data sets for experiments. The model can also notify users of new additions to the database that may be of interest, based on previously defined interest profiles.
4. *Augmented print.* This model addresses variable distribution rather than variable publication. It seeks to exploit various media according to their greatest advantage for a particular user (e.g., a print publication with electronic archives, or an electronic publication with printed archives).

The economics that pertain to electronic publishing are not well known. These models are mainly hypothetical ones with very little experience amassed, thus far, to attest to those that are likely to be the most successful under various conditions. The reordering of economic relationships suggested by these models, however, points to more profound differences between print and electronic publishing than originally imagined. These differences are better understood in the context of the *integrative capacity* of digital electronics.

DIGITAL INTEGRATION

Heretofore, our focus has been on the type of publishing possible in print: namely, the representation of characters and images on paper. We have examined ways in which this type of printing may be replicated in an electronic medium. Electronic publishing, however, also involves the integration of digital components that either cannot be represented on paper or can be represented only at considerable cost. These include such components as high-resolution graphics, color, or program code (which can be represented on paper), as well as animation, sound, dynamic visualizations, or interactive linkages (which are not easily representable on paper).

Competing in a publishing environment in which the arts (text, images, sound, and performance) can be represented in a unified electronic medium has proven to be a daunting challenge. Success involves an element not heretofore discussed: the building of an electronic infrastructure.

The Digital Electronic Infrastructure

The benefits of electronic publishing—while perhaps not immediately perceived within the publishing industry itself—were nevertheless quickly understood to be important by scientists and engineers who had need for the capabilities that electronics provided: (1) rapid and timely communication, (2) communication of multiple representational forms in a single medium (text, images, sound, and animation across digital electronic networks), (3) collaboration over distance and time, and (4) increased local control.

Accordingly, emphasis was placed on enhancing network connectivity and on developing network-savvy applications and management tools. In the wake of this emphasis, came new strategies for distributing network governance, information resources, and fiscal investments. The resulting "matrix" follows entirely new structural dynamics and may one day prove to have been prototypical for larger human organizational changes that are presently evolving.

In its simplest form, the matrix is an outgrowth of a bold investment on the part of the U.S. government to link together its remote national scientific laboratories, some military installations, and certain universities through an electronic network. Its formal beginning, evolution, and present state are best detailed in Charles Quaterman's text, "The Matrix."[4] For the sake of this discussion, the infrastructure that presently exists is widely known as the Internet. The Internet is growing at a phenomenal rate (25 percent per month, compounded),[5] which means that several million computers (and via those computers, even more individuals) are now interconnected on a worldwide basis. From a publishing point of view, several very important characteristics derive from this infrastructure:

- ubiquity of access
- common language
- economies of scale
- integrated products
- new opportunities
- subsidiary markets for existing products

- increased competition from unexpected sources
- new business models

There are considerable and interesting developments within distributed network infrastructures (both at the management and the end-user levels) that may be expected to have an ongoing influence on publishing. These include various compression technologies and mechanisms for improving the transmission of higher volumes of information across existing network channels. These will be accompanied by technological advances permitting wider channels of communication (broadband networks). The integration of fax and cable technologies will signal a unification of otherwise isolated industries. This will provide stimulus for investment, but will also trigger modification in rights and information policies. Harnessing of hypertextual linkages and other navigation and searching tools will improve access and reduce the risk of economic disenfranchisement. These will come about with a parallel development in intelligent agents, artificial intelligence components, natural language commands, and voice- and touch-sensitive hardware—all of which will be designed to provide more ubiquitous access to information. Meanwhile, monitoring and filtering agents will develop to help distinguish useful information from the chaos of disordered and meaningless information. Implications of the worldwide exchange of data will begin to be felt simultaneously in educational and economic arenas. Distribution of needed resources for varying requirements will be enhanced.

All these changes in infrastructure portend (for the optimist) a time when much of human knowledge and scientific discovery may be developed, portrayed, and stored on networks to which many people will have access. This will mean that people can search, retrieve, and use whatever information they may find valuable, in whichever form and in whatever granularity (level of detail) they may wish. Even in the saying, this portends fundamental changes in the publishing activity.

Who Will Be the Publishers of Tomorrow?

Having access to an audience composed of individuals familiar with computers, and capable of using them, is a novelty in the world. Addressing such an audience, and providing it with information and services, are perceived to be a huge potential business. A large proportion of costs associated with print publishing is consumed by delivery and transport expenses. These costs could be substantially reduced, if not virtually eliminated, within a networked environment.

The types of "publications" possible in a digital electronic milieu, as has already been noted, are likely to be more robust—including sound and motion, as well as text and graphics. Manipulable data might be available for certain scientific papers. One's curiosity, whetted by a particularly stimulating paper, could be satisfied by requesting delivery of additional materials on the same subject.

Several things that have already been learned about networked environments bear consideration. The first is that the network is essentially bidirectional. This means that information will not necessarily flow exclusively *from* the publisher *to* the customer. One should anticipate a more active role on the part of the consumer. Transactions are likely to be of several kinds, simultaneously, with some of the entities switching roles. Robert Kost explored these mutable and simultaneous functions in a paper delivered to the Library of Congress some years ago, in which he suggests variable mechanisms for remunerating participants on the network, depending on whether—in a given transaction—they were acting as "originator," "distributor," or "consumer."[6] Each of these functions might have attached to it particular debits or credits, depending on whether one was originating information, merely passing it along, or ultimately using it.

TELECOMMUNICATIONS COMPANIES

Such transactional discrimination requirements lead easily to a major unsolved component of networked information: the billing mechanisms. Currently, there exists much debate as to the role of public utilities, such as phone companies, in the evolving information network. After all, the lines across which most information will travel are likely to belong to telephone companies, whether the lines are a twisted pair of copper cables, or fiber-optic cables that can carry larger amounts of data simultaneously. The phone company also has a very finely tuned billing system already in place for millions of households. It could be, some suggest, that phone companies might play a major role as publishers of the future, because of their ownership of two important elements of infrastructure: communication cables, and billing mechanisms. The courts have generally discouraged allowing the provider of the channel of communication to also become the provider of data traveling along the channel, but the courts might be persuaded to change their opinions if enough stakeholders supported the idea.

Cable Television Vendors

Others are betting that cable television will play an important role in what some are calling the "infotainment" industry. Arguments in favor of cable television include the fact that these vendors will have broadband capability, through which can be introduced into the home interactive programs that appear similar to television programs but that exploit television's potential for engaging audiences. The fact that there is already a socially acceptable form of providing advertising revenue (through commercials) in place is not lost on proponents of cable television operators as the future electronic publishing giants.

Software Developers

Microsoft Corporation is banking heavily, it is said, on multimedia applications for desktop computers. Microsoft has already—in partnership with American, European, and the Japanese electronics giants—established a multimedia standard, hoping to avoid the costly incompatibilities that plagued the computer industry in its infancy. Such a standard permits concurrent development by each of the vendors involved, who know that products they develop are likely to be compatible with one another. This also satisfies an important consumer demand. Consumers like the free-market choice of buying this CPU, that monitor, someone else's disk drive, and another's loudspeakers. If multimedia developers succeed in bringing to market components that are as compatible as stereo audio equipment is, many consumers will be very pleased.

Microsoft announced in 1992 that it had purchased a large interest in a U.K. publishing firm, Dorling-Kindersley. Many analysts wondered why. Yet it is abundantly clear that for successful electronic publishing, one needs command over not only equipment, cables, accounting functions, or marketing acumen but, perhaps most importantly, huge amounts of useful information (content). Microsoft may have been wanting to gain experience with a successful publisher, noted for its pictorial and encyclopedic publications. It may also have wanted to gain access to illustrative materials *at the point of creation*. This chapter has already alluded to the confusion surrounding intellectual property rights. Such confusion is no less common with illustrations that appear in publications. Whether a publisher who owns print reproduction rights also owns the rights to display those images on a screen is not always clear. If a publisher commissions photography or illustrations, the problem of ownership does not exist.

If such images are to appear in multimedia presentations, the single image reproduced in a printed volume may be insufficient. A whole *sequence* of images may be needed to represent, dynamically, what is hinted at through a static image in a printed book. One can imagine, therefore, that the major computer software firms may be the successful publishers of tomorrow, especially if they start financing and developing pedagogical and school-use applications for broad commercial distribution among primary and secondary schools.

HARDWARE MANUFACTURERS

Similarly, hardware manufacturers may enter the electronic publishing field. Steve Jobs bundled a number of informational and reference texts, in CD-ROM format with his NeXt computer releases. This was in acknowledgment, perhaps, of the fact that the world's best computer is likely to be poorly used if there do not exist intellectually challenging things to do with the machine both professionally and for leisure. Social scientists predict that the boundaries between our work and our leisure worlds are likely to be increasingly blurred. If this is so, then both entertainment and professional functions may be served by consumer electronics goods that are brought to market. For this to work well, both passive and intellectually stimulating materials will need to be packaged with expensive hardware. Will the hardware manufacturers become publishing entities, too?

TRADITIONAL PUBLISHERS

The entities mentioned above are nontraditional publishers, it is true. Yet it should be clear that each has some vested interest in pursuing a strategy that brings it closer to what we think of as traditional publishing activities. Earlier, it was noted that McGraw-Hill had already formed links with college bookstores, with McGraw-Hill providing its customers (professors teaching college-level courses) access to McGraw-Hill's database of "textbook chapters." Professors are given the option of selecting some chapters and discarding others, assembling them in sequence, and requesting the inclusion of additional materials (perhaps from the professor's own collection.) In this way, McGraw-Hill hopes to customize textbooks for the particular needs of a professor and a specific class of students. While McGraw-Hill may be providing access to its intellectual database, it has joined in partnerships with college bookstores to actually invest in the necessary printing equipment. In this scenario, then, the traditional functions of manufacturing have been spun away from the publisher, who is relegated to husbandry over intellectual resources and access to these resources. The manufacturing functions can then be assigned to any number of outlets, some of which can produce print on paper versions, others magnetic encoding on disk, and still others optical disk compilations.

MULTIPLICITY OF PLAYERS AND CHANNELS

This last scenario seems most likely to many. Although it reorders relationships, it also capitalizes on expertise in the most efficient manner. At one time, the very physicality of paper and bindings demanded considerable capital investment: both in the creation of printed materials and in their collection. That requirement dictated that mainly large companies and institutions played major roles in publishing efforts, for they alone were able to apply sufficient capital to stoke the enterprise. Today, the combination of an existing communications infrastructure, powerful desktop personal computers, sophisticated software, and specialized narrow-niche interests permit the ingenious and entrepreneurial to play some important role in the function of selecting and disseminating useful and salable information. In addition, the willingness of businesses to increasingly partner with one another to provide specific services means that the options for providing competitive services are wide and profuse. These elements all foreshadow an efflorescence of potentialities in electronic publishing activities, by a wider range of providers than have ever existed before.

PROBLEMS AND CHALLENGES

It is appropriate to conclude this section with a list of identified problems that await some satisfactory resolution before the promise of electronic publishing comes to its fullest fruition.
1. *Billing*. Surely foremost among these is an adequate mechanism for billing. Without this, the economic machinery can scarcely expect to be fueled.
2. *Rights brokering*. Shortly behind the first concern is a need for a stable mechanism for rights brokering and exchange. This has to be automatic and user-friendly. Today, publishers spend an inordinate amount of labor simply managing rights, paying royalties, and protecting interests. If the distributed computer network can be supplied with generalized software mechanisms by which intellectual property rights negotiations and transfers can take place, this burdensome and expensive func-

tion would become generic and transparent.
3. *Quality assurance.* In a time when much less information competed for a reader's interest, the convention of publisher's imprint developed. By this simple means, readers could be assured that certain publications met basic standards of quality. Over time, various imprints became known for particular sorts of expertise. There needs to exist an analog for the publisher's imprint in an electronic publishing environment. It is possible that the imprint of the future may be an electronic reincarnation of personal *mentoring*. Given the discrete pieces of data that can be tracked easily by computers, it might be possible for a user to request a reading list from this or that favorite professor or mentor. This would return the imprint to its original, somewhat personalized status.
4. *Archiving.* One of the functions not deeply explored in this chapter (although it might easily have been included) is the role of libraries and repositories in the wider aspect of publishing. The library, after all, provides ubiquitous access in our society to even the otherwise disenfranchized. It is an essential institution in a democratic society. Libraries also perform important archival functions, retaining—for the record, as well as for future researchers—copies of established literature and resources. The networked environment facilitates publication; that we have seen. Also of concern is the matter of establishing predictable and functional repositories of *fixed* information. Some scholars worry that the dynamic quality of publishable information in the future will preclude archiving and preservation functions currently borne by libraries. It will be important to assure ourselves that these functions also exist in an electronic publishing environment.
5. *Access.* The problem of access is most frequently defined in terms of ensuring access to the disenfranchized. In an electronic milieu, the problem also includes *locating* items of interest. Strategies for ensuring *location* include important architectural developments (e.g., standards for querying remote databases, stable and understandable transmission protocols, consistent database structures, fundamental information requirements). Adequate location parameters also involve considerable information theory (how to make a query, how to implement natural language querying, and how to verify legitimacy

or relevance of responses to queries). Usable location strategies also include consideration of filtering mechanisms (how not to get certain kinds of responses, how to maintain currency without having to repeat a search, and how to discern the wheat from the chaff). Finally, issues of security and privacy abound in this arena: Should we allow encryption of data? Can anyone find out what I've been searching for? Can searches be inspected by outside parties? How can we ensure privacy? Enforce it? When do private interests conflict with public interests in this sphere?

6. *Internationalization.* There is a strong link between access to needed information and personal productivity. Some companies call the provision of adequate information resources to their employees "empowerment," believing that the "empowered" individual, given the necessary tools and information on which to base decisions, can more easily be motivated. There is an expectation that having such motivated and empowered individuals will lead to productivity gains and social achievements, which in turn will translate into economic stability and vitality. Businesses have learned that unlimited growth and exploitation of resources are bound to end in failure. The world's economies are interdependent, and watchwords for the future include such terms as "sustainable growth," and "environmentally responsible businesses." These qualities transfer directly to the electronic environment, where information management must be considered in its global context. "Information rich" countries have important responsibilities to "information poor" countries. The responsibilities include appropriate husbandry of information resources, to be sure; but they also include farsighted visions of how information resources can empower and promote economic stability. It will no longer be possible to act in restricted or local environments. Electronic publishers will need to be consistently cognizant of the global dimensions of their activities and products.

Conclusion

The traditional role of the publisher has been defined by the circumstances of the components with which publishers have worked. Today, publishing is defined as the intelligent act of *selecting* something worthy of publication, and the economic act of *publishing*—that is, making what has been selected available to an appreciative public. The values of authentication, aesthetics, clarification, and marketing are considerable augmentations of information and ideas, provided by the interlocutor, or publisher.

It should now be evident that electronic publishers have a common mandate with their print-based precursors. They also provide similar functional contributions in the act of publication. The differences, however, are radical ones: Electronic publishers must contend with text, graphics, animation, audio, and dynamic interactivity. They also have a variety of outlets, channels of communication, and means of delivery. Economic structures will grow considerably more complex than they are today, likely to involve partnerships with a larger number of discrete partners. Legal and rights issues will be labyrinthine.

Electronic publishers will surely be seen to have evolved from traditional print publishers. They will likely also be so different in their operational and functional roles as to be unrecognizable as members of the same evolutionary limb. What will reveal their common ancestry, however, are the values that both share in common: selecting the most useful and interesting materials, and disseminating them to a waiting public, at a price consistent with the perceived value of their efforts.

Notes

[1] John W. Seybold, *The World of Digital Typesetting* (Media, Penn.: Seybold Publications, 1984).

[2] Stanley Rice, *Book Design: Systematic Aspects* (New York: R. R. Bowker, 1978) and Stanley Rice, *Book Design: Text Format Models* (New York: R. R. Bowker, 1978).

[3] There are many indications of this transformation, perhaps the most advanced expressed by a group of librarians, publishers, and authors, identified as the "Triangle Research Universities' Group," and described in a document written about in the online Internet journal, *Newsletter on Serials Pricing Issues*, edited by Marcia Tuttle (ISSN: 1046–3410), to be found on the Internet at uncvm.1.oit.unc.edu.

[4] Charles Quarterman, *The Matrix: Computer Networks and Conferencing Systems Worldwide* (Maynard, Mass.: Digital Press, 1990).

[5] *The Internet News* (Reston, Va.: Internet Society, 1993).

[6] Robert Kost, "Useright" (presentation at a meeting of the Library of Congress Network Advisory Committee, 24 March 1988), available from author: 445 Hamilton Ave., White Plains, N.Y. 10601.

9

Publishing in the Third World: Issues and Trends for the Twenty-First Century

Philip G. Altbach

The publication of books and other printed material is an important activity in any society. Books stand at the center of the knowledge dissemination systems of all societies. The developing nations of the Third World require books and other printed materials, not only for students to use in schools but for communication at all levels, from the most basic books for literacy to advanced scientific monographs. An independent culture requires books and other printed materials, and Third World countries, which are involved in the highly complex tasks of nation building, have especially urgent needs for published materials.[1]

Despite the predictions of Marshall McLuhan and others, the printed word has not diminished in importance. In the Third World especially, books are central because more sophisticated technologies are often unavailable. Book production and distribution are within the means of most Third World nations, using technologies that are available in most countries. An indigenous publishing industry is at the very center of the process of development. The traditional book has not been eclipsed by new technologies and remains of primary importance.

We are concerned here with the special issues and problems that are involved with publishing in the Third World.[2] While there are many common issues relating to publishing worldwide, and some of these are discussed in this essay, there are a number of specific matters that affect Third World nations. There are also significant variations among Third World nations, and these differences will be highlighted. Africa and Asia will receive the major focus here, as these two regions offer some significant contrasts—with sub-Saharan Africa experiencing severe economic problems that have dramatically affected education and publishing—as well as the lives of people in the region.³ In many ways, Africa has fallen further behind in terms of book development, and there is now a major crisis in terms of both the supply of adequate numbers of books in schools and to the society and in the development of a viable publishing industry in most countries.

In sharp contrast, much of Asia has done relatively better both in terms of the development of publishing and of economic and infrastructural growth. There are, however, major differences between Pakistan and Bangladesh, on the one hand, and South Korea and Taiwan, on the other. Most Asian countries now have a viable publishing industry. Some, such as China, have centrally planned economies, while most have relied mainly on the free market to develop publishing. And some Asian countries, such as Afghanistan and Laos, have yet to provide adequately for book production. Africa and Asia present useful examples for understanding the development of publishing in the Third World.

The publishing of books and other printed material has never received the attention that it deserves from development specialists, government authorities, or the research community. It has traditionally been assumed that a publishing industry would somehow emerge to meet the needs of modernizing societies. It has been discovered that the development of a publishing apparatus in a society is a highly complex matter, by no means assured simply because there is a need for books. In the early period of development, it is fair to say that the provision of books received virtually no attention. However, educational planners and others discovered that curricula could be developed and schools built, but that did not ensure that the needed textbooks would be available. It was only in 1966 that Robert Escarpit coined the term "book hunger" and called attention to the needs of the Third World in terms of book development.⁴ As a result, books started to receive modest attention from national authorities, development planners, and aid agencies. But publishing remained a low priority, and relatively little was done to focus attention on it as a key part of the development process.

Most Third World nations have not developed a clear policy regarding the development of a publishing industry, and in many cases government policies have actually hindered the creation of a viable publishing community. This can be seen when governments centralize the publication of textbooks or when high tariffs are placed on the importation of paper, printing equipment, or supplies. Foreign aid to publishing has been sporadic, sometimes ineffective, and occasionally even counterproductive.[5] For example, the provision of subsidized books to Third World nations as part of foreign aid programs has often hindered the development of indigenous publishing capacity. Most of the major aid-giving nations have sponsored such programs—including the United States, Britain, and the former Soviet Union.[6] From time to time, private foundations have also taken an interest in book development. Some of their programs have been effective, but most have been unsustained and uncoordinated, and few donor agencies have consistently supported book development.[7]

The Importance of Indigenous Publishing

It is our argument that all but the smallest countries need an indigenous publishing industry and the ability to produce the books and periodicals that they need. It is simply not advisable to rely on imported books. Publishers in other countries—and particularly the multinational firms in the industrialized nations—cannot be counted on to meet local publishing needs. The key concepts here are autonomy and indigenization. Publishing is closely linked to culture and to education, and these are deeply rooted in national goals. Books provide access to ideas, and are particularly crucial where the other elements of the mass media, such as television, may be limited. Books are "low-tech" and relatively inexpensive and easy to produce and within the capability of most countries. Publishing is a key means of communicating a culture, and there must be close links between cultural and educational development, on the one hand, and the means of communicating (i.e., publishing) on the other.

Indigenous and autonomous publishing is especially important in the context of the Third World. Many Third World nations are in the process of modernizing or reinterpreting their cultures. The means of communicating these insights is of special importance. Developing countries are also creating new educational systems and the curricula to be used in the schools. Again, there must be an effective means of publishing the textbooks and other reading materials needed for educational systems. Markets for books are generally small. Populations are sometimes small and rates of literacy often low. Further, incomes may be limited, and frequently no tradition of purchasing books exists. In many Third World nations, a high proportion of the population lives in rural areas and has no access to books or other published material. There are, therefore, special needs to be met by publishers. The creation of a publishing industry under such unfavorable conditions is, of course, a significant challenge.

Yet, books are a key part of national development, and it is simply not enough to have access only to imported books, which were created abroad, for different purposes. Third World nations require books that reflect their emerging needs, which only they can determine. For example, there is widespread demand for printed material in local languages to provide the basis for sustained literacy and access to the national culture for the largest possible segment of the population.

The development of an indigenous publishing industry, even of modest proportions, is within the capability of most Third World countries. Publishing is neither high-tech nor high-cost, particularly when compared to other "infrastructural inputs." Coordination of the manifold elements involved in producing books is needed—from the editorial and managerial expertise of the publisher to printing and paper and the apparatus of distributing books. In the Third World, governments must be involved in the process to ensure that capital will be available for investment, to permit the import of machinery and paper if needed, and to provide the atmosphere in which a book industry can develop.[8]

Publishing as an International Phenomenon

Publishing is an international phenomenon, and the development of a publishing industry in one country cannot be separated from international factors. This is true in the large industrialized nations, where the expansion of multinational publishers has made publishing a truly international business. Huge firms like Elsevier, Bertelsmann, and Hachette are active in publishing in many countries, including a growing number of Third World nations. The traditional power of metropolitan publishers in the Third World remains strong as well.

New technologies affect publishers everywhere. New databases permit sharing of bibliographical and other information concerning books worldwide, and new "on-line" bibliographic and reference services are available in many countries. Innovations in composition, generally using computer technology, are affecting publishing worldwide. "Desktop" publishing has revolutionized scientific publishing and has had an impact both in the industrialized nations and in some Third

World nations. The new technologies are a special challenge to the Third World, since they originate in the West and often require highly sophisticated personnel and infrastructures. Nonetheless, this is a period of unprecedented technological change in publishing.

Trends in copyright have international implications. Knowledge is increasingly an international commodity without boundaries, and copyright is the arrangement that regulates the international flow. Book exports and imports are an important part of publishing worldwide. Britain, for example, exports a significant part of its book production. American publishers, while they export fewer books, actively sell rights to foreign publishers. Many Third World nations import most of their books, sometimes including school textbooks, from abroad.

Third World nations do not control the international environment of publishing. They are basically dependent on the industrialized nations.[9] The decisions made in the industrialized nations regarding copyright, the import and export of books, the prices of products—such as computer-based composition equipment—and even the international price of paper are all determined in the industrialized nations. The international copyright apparatus is controlled by the industrialized nations.[10] Decisions made by the dominant powers in the knowledge network are made, in general, with their own interests in mind and without regard to the needs of the Third World. The industrialized nations are, of course, not trying to weaken Third World book development. It is simply that the interests of publishers in the West do not always coincide with that of their compeers in the Third World. There are clearly significant inequalities in the international publishing equation, and the Third World cannot act with full autonomy in terms of book development and publishing. The structural impediments to autonomous publishing development must be fully understood in order to deal with an industry that is by its very nature international.

The traditional role of Western influence on Third World publishing stems in part from the heritage of colonialism. In those parts of the Third World that were under colonial domination until fairly recently, and this includes much of Africa and Asia, the impact of colonialism often remains significant. The colonial power determined the nature of the development of publishing in the country as well as the shape of the modern educational system. The French generally preferred to publish books in France and export them to their African colonies, leaving Francophone Africa without significant publishing capacity at the time of independence. The British, in general, pursued a more laissez faire policy and permitted indigenous publishing to develop although they did not encourage it. British firms also entrenched themselves in the colonies, often dominating the most important market for books—the school textbook market.[11] In some cases, expatriate firms continue to be important in local publishing, while in others, such as India, governmental action forced foreign companies to sell a majority control to local people.

Patterns of commerce established in the colonial period continue to be important, and these affect publishing. Commercial links, for example, tend to run between Africa and Europe rather than among African nations. Thus, it is even now often easier for book buyers in Nigeria to obtain books from Britain than from Kenya or Tanzania. Similar colonially based patterns of book exports remain significant—until recently, commercial agreements gave the British virtual domination over their former colonies, and it is still the case that most books purchased from overseas in Anglophone Africa come from Britain. France is even more dominant in Francophone Africa. The expatriate firms, in general, no longer monopolize publishing and book sales, but they remain extremely powerful. In many Third World countries, American firms have joined with those from the former colonial power.

Language is one of the most important elements in Third World publishing, and one that is, in significant ways, linked to the heritage of colonialism. The language of the colonizer generally became the dominant language of the colony. Used for government, the legal system, commerce and, perhaps most significantly, for education, the colonial language naturally became the main language of intellectual life and of books. The dominance of the colonial language continued after independence, and in almost every former colonial area, the issue of language remains controversial and of primary importance to education publishing and the nation's intellectual life.

Of course, colonialism was not the only factor influencing language policy and development in the Third World. In some countries, mainly but not exclusively in Africa, Western languages were retained after independence for both political and demographic reasons. A proliferation of local languages made the choice of a primary language very difficult. In some cases, these indigenous languages were spoken by very small populations, and many were without written forms.[12] Even where local languages were an option, political disputes often prevented decisive action. The politics of language in the Third World is a powerful force—sometimes leading to civil unrest. For example, there has been continuing opposition in India to using Hindi as the sole national language. English remains a key language for commerce, politics, and intellectual life—forty years after independence close to half the books published in India are in English—and English almost completely dominates scholarly and scientific publishing and much of political analysis.[13] Other countries, including Indonesia and Malaysia, moved decisively to use indigenous languages as the main media for education and publishing, and while these shifts have not been without problems they have been successfully accomplished.

Language is a part of the international equation in publishing. The link is obvious where a metropolitan language is widely used in publishing. But there are other aspects of language that play a role as well. The bulk of the world's books are published in Western languages—and the phenomenon is even greater for scientific and technical books. Thus, many Third World nations must import a significant segment of their book needs from abroad—almost always in Western languages. Further, there are many translations of books from one nation to another. The very large proportion of translations are from the major Western languages to other languages. For example, of a total of 55,618 titles translated in 1983, 41,740 were originally written in just four languages—English (with close to half of the world's total), Russian, French and German.[14] The largest Third World translation source language was Arabic, with only 322 titles. Surprisingly, only 148 titles were translated from Chinese into other languages. These statistics are significant for several reasons. They indicate that the flow of knowledge and information is almost exclusively one-way—from the industrialized nations to the Third World and that creative and scientific work done in Third World languages seldom reaches an international audience. It is also true that the countries and publishers that are the source of translations control the price and the flow of translated materials for the most part. While little is known about how decisions are made regarding which books are translated and how the translation process works, this is clearly an important part of the publishing equation in the Third World and one of the key international elements in this equation.

Knowledge is expanding rapidly, perhaps at an unprecedented rate. This expansion has special implications for the Third World. A very large proportion of the expansion is taking place in the industrialized nations. The bulk of the world's scientific research and publication is done in the West. Virtually all of the world's scientific publications emanate from the industrialized nations—the Third World uses scientific information but produces very little of it. The Third World must import its science—and often pays a high price for it.[15]

Even where scientific research takes place—as in India, which may be considered the Third World's scientific "superpower"—this knowledge is not adequately communicated to other countries, since Indian journals are not widely used or cited outside of India.[16] Third World nations are at a significant disadvantage when it comes to both the production and the utilization of science, since they must import knowledge from the West and they have little control over the channels of communication. While scientific publishing is only a small part of the total publishing industry, it is a very important element—and one that is generally ignored in analyses of publishing.

Copyright

Copyright controls the international flow of knowledge and is of considerable significance in any discussion of Third World publishing.[17] Indeed, copyright has been one of the most controversial and acrimonious of issues. Copyright has often divided publishers in the Third World and in the industrialized nations, but basic interests and concerns differ significantly. The main international copyright agreements—the Berne Convention, sponsored mainly by the European nations, and the International Copyright Convention (ICC), initiated after World War II by the United States—basically reflect the interests of the "have" countries, which produce and control knowledge. Many in the Third World have argued that the interests of development and of justice would be served by significant alterations in the copyright agreements to give more leeway for developing countries to freely copy or translate material.[18] In the 1970s, some modest changes in the copyright agreements were implemented in an effort to meet some of the demands of the developing countries, but even these were not fully ratified and were in many cases compromises that pleased neither group.

It is significant that in the past decade Third World views on copyright have changed. There are very few Third World critics who now favor scrapping the entire copyright system—at one time there were quite a few opponents of the overall structure. India, which was a strident critic of the system, now finds itself an exporter of books and other copyrighted materials and has become a supporter of copyright. Many countries that at one time had very weak copyright laws or no laws at all and were engaged in piracy of books, computer software, and other items have joined the system and curtailed or eliminated piracy.[19] Singapore, Taiwan, South Korea, Indonesia, and Malaysia now generally adhere to copyright regulations, at least with regard to books and published material. Only Thailand still seems to be a hotbed of piracy, and this more in terms of computer materials and trademark products than books. The promulgation of the first copyright law in China in 1990 has meant that the last major holdout has moved to join the copyright community.

Third World nations have joined the international copyright system for several reasons. The industrialized nations have applied major pressure in terms of threats of trade sanctions and other penalties—they were more concerned with violations concerning films, computer software, and trademarked consumer products than with books, but books were included as well.[20] The major noncomplying nations have developed their own publishing industries; some are now exporting books or other printed material and feel that in the long run participation in the copyright system regularizes both the domestic book industry and international commerce. These countries need to import not only books and journals but also scientific equipment and software, and participating in the copyright system is useful for trade relations. In short, the cost of noncompliance became too high.

The fact remains, however, that the international copyright system favors the "haves" and increases both the cost and the complexity for Third World countries. It is in the short-term best business interest of the major Western publishers to keep the copyright system rigid and to operate it on purely commercial terms. The Western publishing community, in general, has taken a "hard line" on copyright issues and has been reluctant to modify the rules or even bend them significantly. In terms of textbooks, scientific materials, and creative writing, it would be a significant contribution to development to provide easier access to materials, to translation and reprint rights, and in general to knowledge products from the industrialized nations to the Third World. Granting such access to the low per capita income countries would not be a serious financial drain on the industrialized nations.

Third World Issues

There are, of course, many common elements in publishing worldwide. Indeed, there are more similarities among nations than differences. Yet, there are aspects of the publishing equation that have special ramifications for the Third World. One of these is copyright, which has already been discussed. Copyright illustrates the interrelatedness of many of these topics—the fact that Third World publishing has strong and usually dependent relationships with the international knowledge network. It is our purpose here to highlight some of the key issues that affect Third World publishing after several decades of development in which a variety of approaches have been taken in different countries. These issues are illustrative of broader concerns and relationships as well as being important in their own right.

PAPER

Paper is a necessary ingredient in publishing. Without it, there are no books. Yet, Third World nations are at a distinct disadvantage when it comes to paper. Most Third World countries do not produce a sufficient amount of the "cultural paper" needed for book production, and many produce virtually no paper at all. Thus, supplies of cultural paper must be imported in a market that is dominated by several major industrialized nations (notably Canada and Sweden) as producers and by major Western user countries (such as the United States), which set prices.[21] Further, the large Western multinational publishers and other major users in the industrialized nations can obtain paper less expensively by purchasing in bulk. While the price of paper has been relatively stable in the past decade, this has not always been the case, and prices are determined by the Western users and producers. There have been some discussions of the possibilities of using paper made from products indigenous to the Third World, and modest progress has been made in this area.[22] There has been consideration of establishing "paper banks" and other coordinated schemes to ensure supplies of cultural paper to developing countries. Some Third World nations have invested in paper producing facilities and have increased domestic supplies. In some cases, newsprint, which is less expensive and more frequently available domestically, has been used for books in Third World countries—thus reducing both cost and dependence on foreign suppliers. Governmental policies, however, sometimes work against ensuring adequate paper supplies, often by imposing high tariffs on cultural paper—somehow assuming that it is a luxury item—or by preventing the development of domestic paper production capacity.

Several foreign assistance agencies, most notably the Canadian Organisation for Development through Education (CODE), have established programs to provide paper to Third World nations at subsidized prices.[23] In terms of the total cost of production of books, paper is a significantly larger element in the Third World than in the industrialized nations, and it is likely to be imported and therefore subject to import controls and the vagaries of the international marketplace.[24] Its supply is uncertain and its price fluctuating. Yet, paper is a requirement for book production; consequently, those involved in the publishing process, from government agencies formulating overall trade and investment policies to publishers and distributors, must take the nuances of paper supply and usage into consideration.

TEXTBOOKS

The fact is that the provision of school and university textbooks is the largest single element of publishing in Third World countries. Even in the industrialized nations, textbooks constitute a significant part of the publishing equation—in the United States accounting for approximately one-fourth of the total industry. In the Third World, it is fair to say that textbooks come close to dominating publishing. Not only are the book needs of the educational system immense, but other markets tend to be limited. Textbooks have received remarkably little attention until recently in discussions of Third World publishing, despite their dominant position.[25]

While it is not possible to discuss all of the elements of textbook publishing here, several issues are important to consider in a broader analysis of Third World publishing. Of considerable importance, of course, is the challenge of developing and providing textbooks to rapidly expanding educational systems. The problem is not simply one of printing and distribution but often of creating suitable books in a context where nothing at all exists. Educational expansion has been a priority of every developing nation, and textbooks are a key part of the provision of schooling—contributing significantly to the success of the educational enterprise.[26] There is a need to create books in indigenous languages and from an indigenous perspective.

Because textbooks are such a large part of the total publishing enterprise, it is important to coordinate textbook development with the broader needs of the publishing industry as well as of the educational system.[27] There has been a tendency in the Third World for textbooks to be developed and published by government agencies, even where texts were previously published in the private sector. The reasons for this are evident: the desire to ensure that book development and creation—often done in government agencies or by government-sponsored organizations—are directly linked to production; the desire to keep prices low by directly controlling printing and production; a distrust of the private sector, which was often dominated by foreign firms; and a wish to maintain direct control over the scheduling and distribution of books. Where books are distributed free to pupils, the tendency to move to government publishing has been particularly strong. Government involvement in textbook publishing was also related to the tendency in the Third World for the public sector to dominate the economy.

Government textbook publishing often achieved its goals, but there are a number of questions that must be raised. It is very clear that government control of the most important—and the most financially predictable and often most profitable—segment of the publishing enterprise takes from the private sector its most lucrative element. Even in industrialized nations, textbook sales often subsidize publishing of less profitable kinds of books. Without the text market, private Third World publishers may have insufficient business to maintain full-scale publishing activities. Government textbook publishing agencies are sometimes inefficient. While there are no convincing cross-national data on this topic, there is a good deal of evidence to indicate that highly subsidized state-run textbook units operate less efficiently than other publishing organizations.

Policies with regard to textbooks have remained controversial and subject to debate. For example, the question of whether texts should be provided free of charge or whether students should pay for their books has been argued with no fully satisfactory response. Questions of textbook design and physical quality also remain actively debated. Some argue that textbooks should be cheaply printed and not expected to last, while others advocate the general Western practice of printing very durable textbooks that are expected to be used for a number of years. And, as noted above, there are arguments concerning whether the public or the private sector—or some combination of the two—should be responsible for textbook publishing. There is general agreement that multinational firms should not dominate a Third World textbook market and that the books, insofar as possible, should not be imported. It is also generally agreed that textbooks and instruction, at least in the elementary grades, should be in the mother tongue of the pupil.

In many countries, there is a severe shortage of textbooks. While there is still some disagreement among experts concerning the appropriate ratio of books to pupils, it is clear that by any measure there are massive shortages of books. Textbook development is a complex process, involving not only publishers but also educational experts and requiring the coordination of the education system, government agencies, and the publishing community. A significant amount of time is required for the development, evaluation, and publication of texts. The World Bank, through its lending program to a number of countries, has addressed the textbook shortage—it has recognized the need to rapidly expand the supply of textbooks.[28]

Several things seem clear. There is a need for educators, governments, and publishers to develop workable strategies to improve the supply of textbooks in the Third World. It is important for textbooks to be integrated into the broader publishing industry so that publishers can obtain some economic benefits from textbooks—only in this way can a balanced publishing program be built. There are many different kinds of textbooks, and an appropriate textbook strategy must take these variations into consideration. For example, the texts needed for postsecondary education are of a different type than those required at the elementary and secondary levels. Supplementary school materials need additional attention. Clearly, textbooks are a crucially important segment of the Third World publishing equation—a segment often ignored in discussions of publishing.

DISTRIBUTION

It is universally agreed that book distribution is one of the most difficult problems for publishing—not only in the Third World, but in virtually every country.[29] But for the Third World, book distribution must be seen as a top priority. The Third World faces some special problems. Low income, largely rural populations are not in a position to purchase books. Nor do they have access to bookstores. Some countries have attempted to use mobile book shops in rural areas, but in general, rural populations remain severely underserved. Bookshops in the Third World are generally inadequate. They do not have large stocks of books, and they are, in general, severely undercapitalized. Booksellers—as well as publishers—find it difficult to obtain credit, and they can afford to keep only small numbers of books in their shops. The discount structure for publishing does not permit adequate profits for booksellers. Endemic Third World problems of transportation add to the burden of book distribution.[30] It has often been said that the book distribution network is the weakest link in the Third World publishing equation.³¹

IMPORTS AND EXPORTS

The Third World relies to a considerable extent on imported books. Small countries and some larger nations without a significant publishing industry must import most, if not all, of their books. Even large countries with active indigenous publishing industries, such as India, import large numbers of books from abroad. For many Indian publishers, there is more profit in importing and selling foreign books than in producing domestic titles. The Third World will always have to rely on imported books and periodicals in the sciences. A number of questions must be raised concerning book imports.

- Why is the cost of foreign books so high in the Third World? There might be a possibility of consolidating orders and thus reducing costs. Industrialized country publishers have claimed that their risks are high and that they therefore must charge more.
- Should more books be reprinted in Third World countries under license from the original Western publisher? Special inexpensive editions of university textbooks published by several American publishers have been available for many years. Should such programs be expanded? What are the implications, in financial terms, for both the originating and reprinting publisher?
- What are the implications of book imports for indigenous Third World publishing? Do imported books take market share from domestically published volumes? Does the import trade, which is part of the business of many Third World publishers, significantly help those publishers to survive in a difficult economic environment?
- How can imports be discouraged and indigenous publishing be advanced without at the same time restricting access to information?

For an increasing number of Third World nations, book exports have become a significant part of the publishing equation. The publishing giants of Latin America, Argentina, and Mexico have long relied significantly on book exports to other Latin American countries.³² Brazil now exports books to Portugal and other Lusophone countries. In recent years, India has become a major exporter of books in English to Southeast Asia and Africa, largely for use as textbooks.[33] An indication of the importance of the export market for Indian publishers is the fact that decisions regarding the publishing of scholarly books in India are in part determined by an estimate of the export potential for a title.[34] Egypt has traditionally served as the major publishing center for books in Arabic, exporting books in large numbers to other Arabic-speaking countries.[35] Singapore and Hong Kong have become key international centers for composition and printing and, to a more limited extent, for publishing. Their up-to-date equipment could be more frequently used for Third World publishing.

Despite some successes, it is typically very difficult for Third World books to be sold in the industrialized nations, and just as difficult to reach audiences in other developing countries. Several efforts at regional Third World publishing cooperation have failed. There are, at present, restrictions on the flow of books between Malaysia and Indonesia, despite the use of a common indigenous language. Efforts in both East and West Africa to promote regional cooperation have not been notably successful. The recently established African Books Collective (ABC) is one of the most significant efforts in recent years to ensure that books published in sub-Saharan Africa reach audiences outside the country of publication.[36]

The importance of making indigenous books available throughout the Third World cannot be overemphasized, for reasons of economics and also in order to promote South-South dialogue. At the same time, the industrialized nations are significant purchasers of Third World books now, and this market can be expanded. Typically, libraries and other institutional purchasers prefer to buy from outlets in their own countries, and it may be useful to expand stocklists and in other ways to make books available to Western purchasers. A few agencies have been developed, in the industrialized nations, to assist in this process. Several outlets, for example, distribute books from India, and at least one specializes in books from the Philippines. For both domestic use and for export purposes, the improvement of bibliographical sources for new Third World books will be very useful. The *African Book Publishing Record* has already made an important contribution in this area.

NEW TECHNOLOGIES

The advent of new technologies for composition, reprography, printing, networking, and storage is perhaps the most important set of developments in publishing in the past two centuries. The new technologies have significant implications for the Third World. In 1975, Datus Smith wrote about the "bright promise" of publishing in developing countries, arguing that new technological innovations in publishing would permit the Third World to leap-frog existing technologies and hasten book development.[37] While it is true that some of the new technological innovations have assisted publishing development in the Third World, it can be argued that these innovations have created as many problems as they have solved. It must be kept in mind that the new technologies have been developed in the West for Western use by Western companies. In many ways they have solidified Western domination of the international knowledge network.[38] The current challenge is for the Third World to fully understand the implications of the new technologies and to carefully make choices concerning their use and role in indigenous publishing.

It is useful to catalog some of the new technologies from the perspective of their impact on the Third World:

Reprography has permitted Third World users of published materials to photocopy easily, often in violation of copyright guidelines. Until recent vigorous copyright enforcement in Asia, unauthorized photocopying was rampant and unauthorized editions of Western books, using reprographic techniques, were common. Reprography was used in conjunction with photo-offset printing to quickly and inexpensively produce unauthorized editions of many books, from university texts and reference volumes to works of popular fiction.[39] Thus, it is fair to say that the widespread use of photocopying machines—many of them manufactured in Third World countries—has been an advantage to the developing countries.

Databases and computer-based means of knowledge dissemination have been a mixed blessing for the Third World. On the one hand, databases permit users in the Third World to have immediate on-line access to the latest information in most scientific fields. Wealthier Third World nations, such as Singapore and Taiwan, have access to the major international databases. However, databases are expensive, and they require support facilities to provide the information that the databases present. Users must pay for the services and must have the infrastructures to permit the databases to function. Of course, all of the databases originate in the industrialized nations, and they require payment for use. Some are operated by profit-making companies. Third World countries and institutions that cannot afford the databases or that do not have the infrastructures—such as a reliable telephone system and consistent electrical power—cannot link up with the databases, and as a result, they may be more disadvantaged in terms of participation in the international knowledge network than was previously the case. Most African nations and many Asian countries are in this situation. It is also the case that the databases are created largely for Western use and the material that is included does not fully reflect the needs of developing nations.

New printing and composing technologies have also been a mixed blessing for the Third World. As with virtually all high-tech equipment, new printing machines are imported from the industrialized nations—and they are often expensive. In countries where a publishing infrastructure is being newly established, investment in the most up-to-date equipment may be justified. Further, computer-assisted composing equipment may be very useful for scripts, such as Urdu, that do not lend themselves easily to traditional typesetting. It is also possible that short-run books can benefit from computer composition, perhaps creating camera-ready material directly from manuscripts produced on disks. Finally, in countries with small populations and relatively high wages, such as the nations of the Arabian Gulf, the new technologies permit publishing to be done with a small staff.

But it seems clear that the new technologies are not a panacea for the Third World. For many countries where traditional composing and printing is well established, the new technologies may not make economic sense. In India, for example, the existence of relatively low wages combined with skills in the older technologies means that traditional composing and printing still makes economic sense for a large part of the publishing industry. The same is true for China and for many other Third World countries. Labor-saving technologies are not necessarily an economic benefit.

The new technologies may have other disadvantages as well. They all require imported equipment—computers, printers, as well as both "hardware" and "software." This equipment is expensive and must be paid for in hard currency. In many countries, maintenance is a problem, and technical support for complex new computer-based equipment may not be available.

There is considerable pressure to invest in the new technologies. The desire to be modern and up-to-date is strong. Publishers who look to exports to the industrialized nations may be under pressure to use the latest equipment in order to be able to produce books that will be acceptable in the international marketplace. In many cases, adopting the new technologies may be a wise decision—a good investment in the long-run health of the publishing firm and the industry in general. In other cases, a combination of old and new technologies may well suit a particular publisher. In still other instances, traditional technologies may be the most advantageous for the country or the firm. The costs and benefits of technological innovation in publishing must be carefully weighed. The pressures, from donor agencies and from many within the country, will be to move to the new technologies promptly. But care must be taken in considering the implications.

PUBLIC OR PRIVATE

There has been much debate concerning whether publishing should be exclusively in the public sector, what the role of the private sector should be, and in a mixed public-private system, what the appropriate division between the two should be. In the current international economic climate, there is a strong prejudice against public-sector enterprises; in the case of publishing, there seems to be little justification for direct public management of publishing firms. The World Bank, which has lent billions of dollars for textbook development, has often favored government production of textbooks despite its general bias in favor of the private sector. This is surprising since governmental control is often inefficient and always leads to starving indigenous local publishing. The collapse of the centrally planned economies in Eastern Europe has added to the arguments against government-administered publishing.

Many Third World countries, in part because of the international tendency during the 1950s and 1960s to have strong state involvement in the economy at all levels, have had a strong state role in publishing. Third World countries have felt that books are, at least in part, a public resource and that they should be subsidized. This is particularly the case for textbooks. It was often thought that since books were being subsidized, publishing might as well be state controlled. In many parts of the world, state involvement in publishing proved not to be fully successful. State enterprises proved not to be very efficient, waste was endemic, and there was inadequate coordination with other elements of the book trade—such as with distributors. Moreover, many have complained that state control led to state censorship of books.

There has been widespread agreement that publishing was most effectively done when free of governmental bureaucracy. Some experiments were carried out to retain governmental fiscal involvement but to downplay bureaucratic controls. In Africa, experiments with "parastatal publishing" were attempted.[40] These government related but semi-independent firms were given a degree of managerial, substantive, and fiscal autonomy—with the idea that they should be professionally managed. At the same time, they continued to receive funds and sometimes overall direction from the government. Their success, however, was limited, and in many instances they have been abandoned.

In many developing countries, the government is involved with publishing and related issues, and many of these efforts have been highly successful. In India, the National Book Trust, a central government-funded semiautonomous agency, has sponsored a large number of programs—including translations of books from one Indian language to others, the coordinated publication of books for children using common artwork in different language editions, as well as the publication of university-level textbooks and the like.[41] The Dewan Bahasa dan Pustaka (national literature agency) in Malaysia has sponsored the translation of many titles into Bahasa Malaysia, as a means of fostering books in the national language. It has been particularly active in the textbook area to meet the strong demand for indigenous textbooks as Malaysia moved to the national language for education.[42] In Singapore, and in many other Third World countries, a government agency, the Curriculum Development Institute of Singapore develops textbook materials that are then published in the private sector. Governments have provided funds to private-sector publishers and have also established public agencies to implement government book policy.

Government policies also have a direct impact on the publishing industry. Tariffs, duties, and restrictions on imports determine to a significant extent the future of the industry in many countries. High tariffs on paper, for example, may make it virtually impossible to publish books domestically, where locally produced paper is in short supply or unavailable. In some countries, publishing is not formally classified as an "industry" and is therefore unable to obtain certain benefits, including access to bank credit. As noted earlier, the "nationalization" of textbook publishing has had a serious, negative impact on private-sector publishing in a number of Third World nations. Sometimes, government policies implemented for justifiable reasons, from one point of view, have unanticipated negative implications in other areas. Publishing is not well understood by governmental authorities and generally has a low profile—thus the full ramifications of policy are sometimes not understood.

Because government has a pervasive role in society in many Third World nations, its role in publishing has been substantial. It is likely, even in this period of privatization, to continue to be an important part of the publishing equation. Thus, it is especially crucial to determine how government can be most effective in book development so that appropriate use can be made of this powerful—and probably inevitable—force in Third World societies.

Regional Variations: Africa and Asia

It is, of course, an overgeneralization to discuss broad trends in Africa and Asia, since there are so many variations in these two large and diverse continents. Nonetheless, it may be useful to contrast some broad elements in the development of publishing. Such contrasts may be useful in understanding the broader configuration of publishing in the Third World. As a broad generalization, publishing in many Asian countries has "taken off," and the basic infrastructures and capacities are in place.[43] This is most dramatically the case in those Asian countries that have achieved economic success and very high literacy rates—the East Asian newly industrialized countries (NICs). Publishing has also developed impressively in such low per capita income nations as India and China.[44] In contrast, publishing in sub-Saharan Africa has not developed significantly in the past two decades. Indeed, in a few major countries such as Nigeria, publishing may even have moved backward. There are a few bright spots, such as Kenya and Zimbabwe, but in general the economic downturn of the recent past has meant that publishing has been severely constrained.[45]

African Dilemmas

It is possible to summarize some of the problems facing book development in sub-Saharan Africa.[46] Clearly, not all of these issues are relevant in each country, but they are broadly applicable to the region.

The economic crisis of the 1980s has affected every aspect of African society, and has been especially difficult for those segments of the economy dependent on imports, such as book publishing. The combination of low prices on the world market for African exports, the international debt crisis, political instability, overpopulation, and mismanagement has been extraordinarily damaging. World Bank statistics indicate that most sub-Saharan African countries have regressed in terms of per capita income and spending for education and related areas.[47] Economic problems have restricted government spending for textbooks, with harmful effects on the book industry. In fact, the shortage of textbooks in many African countries has reached crisis proportions. Restrictions on imports have meant that paper and other materials needed for publishing are in short supply and very expensive or simply unavailable. The inability to import books and journals has meant that the universities no longer have access to the world's knowledge. In short, the economic crisis has affected all elements of publishing in Africa. It is at the root of most of the other difficulties discussed here. Without an improvement in the basic economic situation, it is unlikely that African publishing will fully regain its initiative—and the current world economic situation does not look promising for Africa.

Language issues are also a handicap in Africa. English and French, and to a lesser extent Portuguese, remain powerful forces in Africa, making the establishment of publishing in indigenous languages very difficult.[48] There are, of course, many reasons for the role of the metropolitan languages in Africa, and these factors are useful in understanding African book development. Both the heritage of colonialism and the presence of the multinational publishers clearly have played a role, but it would be a mistake to blame all problems on these external forces. It is also the case that many African countries have found it impossible to choose an indigenous language for political and tribal reasons.[49] Further, in some countries, there are a large number of languages, each serving only a small population. Many African languages are not well developed for use in publishing as they do not have well-developed grammatical structures and/or agreed spellings. The major East African nations of Tanzania and Kenya have, however, stressed the use of Swahili as an indigenous link language, although English remains very important in publishing and in other areas as well. Swahili is not the dominant language of any indigenous group but is fairly widely used along the African coast. Swahili did not seem to be a direct threat to any ethnic or tribal groups, and yet as a language it has some legitimacy in the region.[50]

A significant number of countries use a European language as the major, or even the only, language of schooling at all levels. The upper levels of education continue to be dominated by metropolitan languages without exception.[51] This creates the need for large numbers of textbooks in these languages and instills among intellectuals a kind of loyalty to them. The metropolitan languages remain the keys to social mobility and participation in the modern sector of all African societies. There is no easy solution to the language dilemma in Africa. While language issues affect publishing in very direct ways, the key factors are much broader.

The infrastructures of publishing are in especially short supply in Africa. At the time of independence, most African countries had few publishing resources. Books were largely imported. The situation has only modestly improved since that time. Paper is mostly imported. Printing facilities are totally inadequate and outdated. The distribution network is limited and virtually nonexistent outside of the large cities—and the few booksellers that exist tend to orient themselves toward imported Western books that are more readily available and yield a larger profit. There are very few trained publishing professionals. It has been very difficult to import machinery, technology, or paper to build up the needed infrastructures, and in the present economic climate, such imports are virtually impossible. In short, there has been little basis on which to build a modern publishing industry.

Indeed, given the existing problems, it is surprising that there has been any progress at all. Nonetheless, there are examples of successful indigenous African publishing enterprises that have been able to establish themselves in difficult circumstances. A number of ventures in Kenya have been tried and a few have succeeded.[52] Zimbabwe, which had a fairly strong infrastructure at the time of independence, has continued to build an effective publishing industry, while even under apartheid there was a significant development of indigenous and critical publishing in South Africa.[53]

The lack of regional cooperation in publishing in Africa has been a deterrent to growth. Africa, more than other developing areas, has small linguistic and tribal groupings that not only make the maintenance of a modern nation-state difficult, but clearly hinder book development. Some of the current national boundaries reflect colonial preferences rather than indigenous desires or logical choices. The major linguistic divisions of the continent—between Francophone and Anglophone areas—transcends national boundaries. Small countries have found it impossible to build up an indigenous book industry.

In this context, regional cooperation would seem to be a logical and desirable choice. In West Africa, regional publishing on the basis of Anglophone or Francophone usage would make sense. In East Africa, cooperation based on the common use of Swahili, or even English, could strengthen publishing. Some efforts were made, mainly in East Africa, but almost without exception unsuccessfully. In some cases, political and economic problems at the national level intervened; in others, local factors were responsible. Despite some failed efforts, it would seem that regional cooperation is a key to publishing success in Africa.

ASIAN DEVELOPMENTS

This discussion will focus on the key factors that have permitted some Asian nations to develop effective publishing industries. While there is significant diversity in Asia, we focus here on the factors that have led to success.[54] China and India are both very large nations with low per capita incomes.[55] These countries still have significant shortages of books, both for educational purposes and for general readers; yet they have achieved significant progress in publishing. Taiwan and South Korea have developed impressively in both economic and educational terms in recent years, and their publishing industries have been part of this process of development. Thus, some of the generalizations indicated here will need to be qualified.

An important element for publishing development is relatively healthy economic growth. The East Asian NICs have seen some of the world's most impressive rates of economic growth in the past two decades, and many other Asian countries have also experienced reasonable growth. Economic turmoil on the Pacific Rim in the late 1990s will mean a slowing of growth but not a reversal of basic trends. While the record for India and China has been mixed, they have shown, overall, steady improvement. Economic growth permits an expansion of consumer demand for books, encourages expenditure for education and related cultural programs by government, individuals, and (where it exists) the private sector. There is a larger and more entrenched urban middle class in many Asian countries. This group tends to have disposable income, enabling its members to purchase books. Foreign exchange is made available for necessary imports. Publishing, of course, is part of the economic equation in any country, and general economic health in turn encourages the growth of publishing as well.

A book industry already existed and was, for the most part, domestically controlled. Active publishing industries had existed in many Asian countries for many decades. It was possible to build on available structures and expertise. In India, there are training programs for publishing professionals, and Asians, in general, have had access to the training programs sponsored by the Asian Cultural Centre for UNESCO in Tokyo.[56] A few Asian countries produce printing equipment, although the most sophisticated machines come from the industrialized nations. While most Asian countries are not self-sufficient in paper, most have some papermaking capacity. The Asian countries that have successfully developed publishing industries generally had printing capacity, managerial and editorial expertise, and many of the other components of a successful book industry.

In most Asian countries, publishing was left largely in the private sector, which has been responsible for virtually all of the growth that has taken place. In the NICs, textbooks were also generally left to private-sector publishers who worked closely with education authorities. These private-sector publishers usually received only limited assistance and subsidy from government.[57] An exception to this pattern is China, which has long recognized the importance of books for education and for development.[58] China's publishing development has so far been exclusively in the public sector and, even with the liberalization of recent years, there is virtually no private publishing in China. Indeed, publishing remains fairly centralized, with the resulting problems of lack of flexibility. The Chinese approach to publishing, as was common in socialist countries, has stressed books as a public good. Substantial subsidies were given to the publishing industry, and the price of books was kept artificially low.

Language issues in Asia are not quite as serious as they are in Africa. For the most part, publishing industries function in the national language of the country, although European languages, mainly English, do play an important role.[59] The number of speakers is generally large enough to support an active publishing industry. Even in multilingual countries, such as India, the populations tend to be fairly large. For the most part, the languages involved have traditions of publishing and established grammatical structures and scripts. In some cases, such as Urdu, there have been composition problems, but recent innovations in computer-based composition has significantly simplified the situation. As noted, some language groups—such as Chinese, Hindi, Bengali—are very large although rates of literacy vary and purchasing power may be limited.

Rates of literacy in Asia are, overall, higher than in Africa, and this is an important factor in publishing. Even in countries with high levels of illiteracy—as in India, where the literacy rate remains under 40 percent—there are large numbers of people who can read and can afford to buy books and magazines. For many Asian countries, literacy levels are similar to those in the industrialized nations, despite lower per capita incomes.

There has been a greater level of political stability in much of Asia than has been the case in Africa, despite such disasters as the cataclysmic Cultural Revolution in China. When there were changes in government, either through the electoral process or by less democratic means, the changes tended to be less violent and disruptive.

These are some of the broader factors that differentiate Asia and Africa. Variations exist in the delimited areas of publishing and education in both regions, but perhaps more importantly, there are significant broader political and economic factors that have contributed to the development of a publishing industry in many Asian countries, while inhibiting similar growth in Africa.

The Lessons of the Past Two Decades

Much has been learned since the 1980s with regard to book development and publishing in the Third World. It is worthwhile summarizing some of the major trends and lessons.

REGIONAL COOPERATION

We have learned that regional cooperation is a very useful concept in Third World publishing—and in fact probably a necessary element for publishing in smaller languages and for limited audiences. It has also been learned that regional cooperation is difficult to implement, and few such ventures have been successful. Nonetheless, it remains an important stragegy.

MARKETING AND DISTRIBUTION

Linked to regional cooperation is the coordinated marketing of books overseas—something the African Books Collective is currently attempting to do. There are no such efforts under way in Asia. Because of the nature of export markets—and particularly the library and institutional markets in the United States and Europe—such coordinated efforts can yield considerable increases in sales for some kinds of books. Book distribution has been recognized as the weakest link in the publishing system. Many of the elements of the distribution system are in need of improvement. In most parts of the Third World, publishers are very lax in providing information about new books; as a result bibliographical control is quite weak. Centralized bibliographical services, including national libraries, are inadequate, and publishers do not provide sufficient cooperation. The network of bookstores, especially outside of the urban areas, is weak, which creates problems for book distribution. Discount structures are sometimes unrealistic. Some interesting and occasionally successful efforts to improve book distribution have been undertaken, but in general distribution remains a serious problem for publishing. Indeed, the lack of adequate distribution has limited the effectiveness of the book industry.

GOVERNMENTAL POLICY

We have learned that government policy is a key factor in determining the success or failure of publishing in the Third World. Policies relating to copyright, photoduplication, textbook production, import and export of books, paper, and the like are crucial to the industry. Frequently, these policies are so poorly coordinated that they actually have been a detriment. The establishment of national book development councils in many Third World nations, an innovation stressed by UNESCO, has provided some coordination in the publishing industry. While publishing is not a large part of any economy, it is nonetheless important to national development and deserves significantly more attention than it has received.

TEXTBOOKS

We have learned that textbooks are central to publishing development in all countries, and especially in the Third World. There, textbooks are the largest segment of the publishing industry. The supply of textbooks is also of primary importance to the success of expanding educational initiatives and the improvement of literacy in the Third World.

TECHNOLOGY

The new technologies have significantly altered books and publishing everywhere. Printing, composition, and photocopying are all areas transformed by the technological innovations. How the new technologies fit into the complex balance of Third World publishing is not yet clear. Considerable attention must be given to the implications of these changes for Third World publishing.

Indigenization

Although difficult to implement in many cases, it is extraordinarily important to ensure that Third World publishing is indigenous—that it is locally controlled and directed (even if there is some foreign ownership), attuned to the needs of the society, and able to reflect cultural and other developments in the country. In some cases, orienting publishing to the local language is part of such an indigenization effort.

Conclusion

Third World publishing is at a crossroads. It has achieved a certain level of maturity in some countries. In others, a book "famine" persists and even grows more severe. Publishing has been buffeted by economic crises, technological change, and the dramatic expansion of knowledge in the industrialized nations. For the most part, inadequate attention has been given to the role of publishing and of books and printed materials in general in the development of the Third World. We have learned a great deal about what works and what may be less successful. We have seen the operation of the international knowledge network and its impact on the relatively dependent countries of the Third World. At the same time, we have seen some Third World publishing industries achieve considerable success. Countries like India now export books and have a well-developed publishing infrastructure. At the same time, however, there are not enough textbooks for school children in India.

In short, Third World publishing presents a very mixed picture. The decade of the 1990s presents an opportune time to look carefully at both the successes and the failures of the postcolonial period. A sufficient amount of time has gone by to carefully and dispassionately assess the situation. A basic aim must be to ensure as much autonomy as possible in an interdependent world. Agencies in the industrialized countries, including foreign assistance programs, multinational institutions such as the World Bank and UNESCO, as well as governments, can provide some assistance. Just as important, they must understand the problems and the possibilities of Third World publishing. Those most involved, the Third World countries themselves, must make—and implement—the basic decisions. The responsibility is considerable. The challenges are substantial. But the endeavor is worthwhile since publishing is at the center of the intellectual and educational development of the Third World.

Notes

[1] Per Gedin, "Cultural Pride: The Necessity of Indigenous Publishing" (paper prepared for the Obor Workshop on Third World Publishing, February 1991).

[2] The term "Third World" is an easy, if not totally satisfactory, means of referring to the nations of Africa, Asia, and Latin America. It is recognized, however, that there are significant variations among these nations and that an increasing number of them are no longer poor and boast high levels of literacy.

[3] The World Bank's recent report on education in sub-Saharan Africa highlights the impact of economic problems on all aspects of intellectual life in those countries. See *World Bank, Education in Sub-Saharan Africa: Policies for Adjustment, Revitalization and Expansion* (Washington, D.C.: World Bank, 1988).

[4] Robert Escarpit, *The Book Revolution* (London: Harrap, 1966). This volume was published by UNESCO, which played a leadership role in the 1960s and 1970s in terms of publicizing and fostering book development in the Third World.

[5] See, for example, Stanley A. Barnett, "American Book Aid: A Critical Assessment of Two Major Programs of the 1950s–1970s" (paper prepared for the Obor Workshop on Publishing in the Third World, February 1991).

[6] For a critique of such programs in the Indian context, see Philip G. Altbach, *Publishing in India* (New Delhi: Oxford University Press, 1975), 62–72.

[7] For an example of current American thinking concerning book exports and book programs abroad, see William M. Childs and Donald E. McNeil, eds. *American Books Abroad: Toward a National Policy* (Washington, D.C.: Helen Dwight Reid Educational Foundation, 1986).

[8] An excellent guide to the various elements needed for developing publishing in the Third World can be found in Datus Smith, Jr., *A Guide to Book Publishing* (Seattle: University of Washington Press, 1989).

[9] For an elaboration of this theme, see Philip G. Altbach, "Literary Colonialism: Books in the Third World," *Harvard Educational Review* 45 (May 1975): 226–36.

[10] Philip G. Altbach, "Knowledge Enigma: The Context of Copyright in the Third World," in *The Knowledge Context* (Albany: State University of New York Press, 1987), 85–112.

[11] Samuel Israel, "The Colonial Heritage in Indian Publishing," *Library Trends* 26 (Spring 1978): 539–52 and Keith Smith, "Who Controls Book Publishing in Anglo-phone Middle Africa?" *Annals of the American Academy of Social and Political Science* 421 (September 1975): 140–50.

[12] See Abul Hasan, *The Book in Multilingual Countries* (Paris: UNESCO, 1978).

[13] Tejeshwar Singh, "Publishing in India: Crisis and Opportunity," in *Publishing in the Third World*, ed. Philip G. Altbach, Amadio A. Arboleda, and S. Gopinathan. (Portsmouth, N.H.: Heinemann, 1985), 111–30. See also Philip G. Altbach, *Publishing in India*.

[14]*Statistical Yearbook, 1989* (Paris: UNESCO, 1989), 7–101.

[15]A partial exception to this situation can be seen in the newly industrializing countries of East Asia, which are expanding their scientific research capability. See Philip G. Altbach et al., *Scientific Development and Higher Education: The Case of Newly Industrializing Countries* (New York: Praeger, 1989).

[16]Eugene Garfield, "Science in the Third World," *Science Age* (October/November 1983): 59–65.

[17]For discussions of the international copyright system, with special relevance for Third World countries, see Edward W. Ploman and L. Clark Hamilton, *Copyright: Intellectual Property in the Information Age* (London: Routledge and Kegan Paul, 1980); Philip G. Altbach, "Knowledge Enigma"; and E. I. Olian, Jr., "International Copyright and the Needs of Developing Countries," *Cornell International Law Journal* 7 (May 1974): 81–112.

[18]For a Third World perspective, see Jaman Shah, "India and the International Copyright Convention," *Economic and Political Weekly*, 31 March 1973, 645–48.

[19]For a discussion of piracy, see David Kaser, *Book Pirating in Taiwan* (Philadelphia: University of Pennsylvania Press, 1969). See also W. Gordon Graham, "The Piracy Picture Worldwide," *Publishers Weekly*, 16 July 1979, 33–34.

[20]Publications such as *Copyright News* provide information concerning the Western view of copyright development.

[21]See Jörg Becker, "The Geopolitics of Cultural Paper: International Dimensions of Paper Production, Consumption and Import-Export Structure" (paper prepared for the UNESCO World Congress on Books, 1982). See also Carl Bergendahl, "The Supply of Cultural Paper in Asia," *Asian Book Development* 10 (March 1979): 4–9.

[22]Mason Rossiter-Smith, "Problems and Alladin's Lamp," in *Publishing in Africa in the Seventies*, ed., Edwina Oluwasanmi, Eva-Maria McLean, and Hans M. Zell (Ile-Ife: University of Ife Press, 1975): 289–96.

[23]Paul Eastman, "The Raw Material: Paper," in *Textbooks in the Developing World*, ed. Joseph P. Farrell and Stephen P. Heyneman (Washington, D.C.: World Bank, 1989): 102–12.

[24]Datus Smith, Jr., *The Economics of Book Publishing in Developing Countries* (Paris: UNESCO, 1976), 16.

[25]For the most comprehensive consideration of textbooks in developing countries from a variety of viewpoints, see Farrell and Heyneman, *Textbooks in the Developing World*. See also Philip G. Altbach and Gail P. Kelly, eds., *Textbooks in the Third World: Policy, Content and Context* (New York: Garland, 1988). Peter Neumann, *Publishing for Schools: Textbooks and the Less Developed Countries* (Washington, D.C.: World Bank, 1980) is a more technical consideration of the topic, as is Douglas Pearce, *Textbook Production in Developing Countries: Some Problems of Preparation, Production and Distribution* (Paris: UNESCO, 1982). Finally, see Philip G. Altbach, "Key Issues in Textbook Provision in the Third World," *Prospects* 13, no. 3 (1983): 315–25 for an overview of the topic.

[26]Stephen P. Heyneman, *Textbooks and Achievement: What We Know* (Wash-

ington, D.C.: World Bank, 1978).

[27]S. Gopinathan, "'And Shall the Twain Meet?': Public and Private Sector Relationship in Textbook Publishing in Less Developed Countries," in *The Need to Read*, ed. S. Gopinathan and V. Barth (Singapore: Festival of Books Singapore, 1989), 221-50.

[28]Pacifico Aprieto, "The Philippine Textbook Project," *Prospects* 13, no. 3 (1983): 351-60.

[29]Amadio A. Arboleda, "Distribution: The Neglected Link in the Publishing Chain," in *Third World Publishing*, 42-55.

[30]For a classic statement of the problems of book distribution, see Artur Isenberg, "Toward Better Book Distribution in Asian Countries," *Indian Book Industry* (August/September 1970): 35-55. See also W. Abegbonmire, "The Hazards of Bookselling in Africa," in *Publishing in Africa in the Seventies*, 47-58.

[31]For a perspective on current U. S. developments, see Center for the Book, *The Future of the Book: Part III—New Technologies in Book Distribution—The United States Experience* (Paris: UNESCO, 1984).

[32]Alberto E. Augsburger, *The Latin American Book Market: Problems and Prospects* (Paris: UNESCO, 1981).

[33]Tejeshwar Singh, "Publishing in India: Crisis and Opportunity."

[34]Abul Hasan, "Indian Books in the World Market," in *The Need to Read*, 251-76.

[35]Nadia A. Rizk and John Rodenbeck, "The Book Publishing Industry in Egypt," in *Third World Publishing*, 96-109.

[36]Hans M. Zell, "Africa—The Neglected Continent," *Logos* 1, no. 2 (1990): 19-27.

[37]Datus Smith, Jr., "The Bright Promise of Publishing in Developing Countries," *Annals of the American Academy of Political and Social Science* 421 (September 1975): 130-39.

[38]Some of these themes are dealt with in Anthony Smith, *The Geopolitics of Information: How Western Culture Dominates the World* (New York: Oxford University Press, 1980).

[39]John F. Baker, "Keeping Up with Copyright," *Publishers Weekly*, 23 June 1989, 18-19; "Copyright Turn-round in Asia," *Anti-Piracy News*, no. 12 (October 1987); Paul Gleason, "International Copyright Conflicts over Books—Part 1: The Problem," *Society for Scholarly Publishing Letter* 9 no. 2, (1987): 1-4.

[40]See S. A. Amu Djoleto, *Books and Reading in Ghana* (Paris: UNESCO, 1985), 10-14. See also Walter Bgoya, *Books and Reading in Tanzania* (Paris: UNESCO, n. d.).

[41]Attar Singh, et al., "National Book Trust," *Round Table* 1 (19 March 1972): 28.

[42]Datuk Hassan Ahmad, "The Role of the Dewan Bahasa dan Pustaka in the Advancement of Indigenous Academic Publishing in Malaysia," in *Academic Publishing in ASEAN*, ed. S. Gopinathan (Singapore: Festival of Books Singapore, 1986), 150-56.

[43]See Shigeo Minowa, *Book Publishing in a Societal Context: Japan and the*

West (Buffalo, N.Y.: Prometheus, 1990) for a Japanese perspective on the development of publishing.

[44]There are, of course, some Asian countries where publishing has not developed impressively for a variety of reasons. Nations such as Afghanistan, which has a relatively small population and several main languages and has been involved in a devastating civil war for a decade, not surprisingly has failed to build up much of a book industry. Similarly, Cambodia has seen its book industry regress in recent years.

[45]Hans M. Zell, "Africa—The Neglected Continent" and Walter Bgoya, "Autonomous Publishing in Africa: The Present Situation," *Development Dialogue*, nos. 1–2 (1984): 83–111.

[46]An excellent overall perspective can be found in Per Gedin, "Publishing in Africa—Autonomous and Transnational: A View From the Outside," *Development Dialogue*, nos. 1–2 (1984): 98–112.

[47]World Bank, *Education in Sub-Saharan Africa*.

[48]Gunter Simon, "The Book in Francophone Black Africa: A Critical Perspective," *African Book Publishing Record*, no. 4 (1984): 209–15.

[49]For a controversial discussion of some of these issues, see Ali A. Mazrui, *The Political Sociology of the English Language: An African Perspective* (The Hague: Mouton, 1975).

[50]It is interesting that the choice of *Bahasa Indonesia* as the national language of Indonesia was based on similar circumstances. This Malay language was not the mother tongue of any of Indonesia's main ethnic groups, and yet it was widely used in the region as a commercial medium.

[51]See S. B. Bankole, "Indigenous Publishing of Tertiary-Level Books in Nigeria: Issues and Problems," *African Book Publishing Record*, no. 4 (1985): 197–200.

[52]See, for example, Henry Chakava, "A Decade of Publishing in Kenya: 1977–1987—One Man's Involvement," *African Book Publishing Record*, no. 4 (1988): 235–41.

[53]David Martin, "Zimbabwe Publishing House—The First Two Years," *African Book Publishing Record*, no. 4 (1983): 181–84 and Peter Randall, "Publishing in South Africa: Challenges and Constraints," *African Book Publishing Record*, nos. 2–3 (1983): 105–09.

[54]It is certainly true that many Asian countries have not developed successful publishing industries. Countries like Nepal or Bangladesh, which have very low per capita incomes, have lagged behind. So have Cambodia and Burma, which have seen years of war or severe economic mismanagement. A few Asian countries, for example Laos or Mongolia, have very small populations and have found the development of indigenous publishing difficult.

[55]It should be noted that even in India, the world's eighth-largest publishing nation, there are significant problems and inequalities. In several of the regional languages, such as Assamese, there is very little publishing taking place while some of the other languages such as Bengali and Marathi have made significant progress. English remains entrenched as a major publishing

language.

[56] Additional seminars were sponsored by Canadian assistance agencies in cooperation with the International Rice Research Institute in the Philippines.

[57] An exception here is India, where textbook publishing at the elementary and secondary levels is in general in the hands of the public sector. This situation has had negative implications for private-sector publishers.

[58] The literature on contemporary publishing in China is very limited. See Fang Houshu, "A Brief Account of Book Publishing in China," in *Publishing in the Third World*, 131–37.

[59] In India, approximately half of the book titles published are in English—although fewer than 3 percent of the Indian population is literate in English. The bulk of book publishing in Singapore is in English, and small segments of publishing in other Asian countries is in English as well.

Contributors

Philip G. Altbach is J. Donald Monan SJ Professor of Higher Education and director of the Center for International Higher Education at Boston College. He is also director of the Research and Information Center of the Bellagio Publishing Network. He is coeditor of *International Book Publishing: An Encyclopedia*, editor of *Publishing and Development in the Third World*, and author of *The Knowledge Context*.

Damtew Teferra is currently a doctoral student in Higher Education Administration at Boston College's School of Education. He has a master's degree in Publishing from Stirling University, Scotland. He has published on African scholarly journals and significantly contributed to the promotion of the African Association of Science Editors—Ethiopian Chapter.

Amadio A. Arboleda is professor at Josei International University, Tokyo, Japan. He has been chief of publications at the United Nations University, and an editor at the University of Tokyo Press. He is coeditor of *Publishing in the Third World*.

Pernille Askerud is a consultant working on publishing issues. Author of *A Guide to Sustainable Book Provision*, she is currently based in Bangkok, Thailand.

Paul Brickhill has been executive secretary of APNET, the African Publishers Network, and director of Grassroots Publishers in Harare, Zimbabwe.

Paul Gleason is an assistant editor with the International Monetary Fund in Washington, D.C. He has served as editor of the *Society for Scholarly Publishing Letter*.

Gordon Graham is editor of *LOGOS*, and has served as chairman and chief executive officer of Butterworths Publishers. He is the author of *As I Was Saying*.

Czeslaw Jan Grycz is a publishing and technology consultant. He has been director of the Scholarship and Technology Study Project, Division of Library Automation, Office of the President, University of California. He is currently a faculty member of the University of Denver Publishing Program.

Datus C. Smith, Jr. is the former director of the Princeton University Press and was founder of Franklin Book Programs, an agency devoted to assisting in the promotion of publishing in developing countries. He has published widely on publishing issues and other related topics.

www.ingramcontent.com/pod-product-compliance
Lightning Source LLC
Chambersburg PA
CBHW070636300426
44111CB00013B/2136